# EVERLASTING
# LIGHT BULBS

ALSO BY JOHN KAY

Culture and Prosperity (USA), 2004
The Truth about Markets, 2003
The Business of Economics, 1996
Why Firms Succeed (USA), 1995
Foundations of Corporate Success,1993
(with M A King) The British Tax System, 1990 (5th edn.)

# EVERLASTING LIGHT BULBS

## How economics illuminates the world

## JOHN KAY

*Illustrations by Roger Beale, Graham Fowell
and Roni Burrell*

*ep*

THE ERASMUS PRESS

First published in Great Britain in 2004 by
The Erasmus Press Ltd
PO Box 4026
London W1A 6NZ

A catalogue record for this book is available
from the British Library

ISBN 0-9548093-0-0

Designed by Briony Chappell

Printed in Great Britain by
Antony Rowe Ltd
Chippenham
Wiltshire

# Contents

# Preface

It was the best of times, it was the worst of times. The essays in this book were written between 1996 and 2003. The period began with Alan Greenspan fearful of 'irrational exuberance': but in the same week *Business Week* announced the arrival of 'the new economy'. The greatest speculative bubble in world history followed. Supporters of the American business model had triumphantly proclaimed 'the end of history' as the Berlin Wall fell. Their self-confidence was reinforced by America's strong economic performance through the 1990s.

But capitalism's triumph was greeted with new attacks on its legitimacy. Demonstrators broke up the Seattle meeting of the World Trade Organisation in 1999 and besieged every subsequent economic summit. The bursting of the stock market bubble was followed by the collapse of once iconic companies such as Enron and WorldCom. The accounting firm Andersen disintegrated. The ball was over.

Or was it? As we put together this collection at the beginning of 2004, the ballgoers, somewhat depleted in numbers, were clustering hopefully at the edges of the room, waiting to take once more to the floor. Massive fiscal and monetary expansions had revived growth in the American economy. The US government's budget deficit was widening rapidly and the country was borrowing from the rest of the world on a scale never seen before. But could the scepticism generated by the collapse of the bubble withstand the desire of everyone – government, financial institutions, businesses and the media – to believe that the story of a 'new paradigm' was true after all?

Those who do not learn from history are destined to repeat it:

but this book is not an economic history of that era of boom and bust. Nor is it primarily a commentary on those extraordinary events, although the background they provided is ever present. Periods such as 1996-2003 are best understood through dispassionate observation. There are enduring truths about how national economies, businesses and industries function: truths valid before 1996, still valid in 2004, and discarded at great danger to our reputations and our wealth.

The book is based on columns which I wrote fortnightly, and more recently weekly, for the *Financial Times*. These are reproduced broadly as they appeared, with minor amendments to increase clarity but not to incorporate hindsight. I am grateful to Richard Lambert, who first asked me to write for the paper, to his successor Andrew Gowers, and to Ed Carr and Andrew Hill, for their support. And to Jo Charrington, Alina Jardine and Kasper Viio for their help in turning the material into the present volume.

# The economics of everyday life

Why does so much modern advertising contain no information about the advertised product? Why should I not have been surprised to encounter an old friend in the remote foothills of the Himalayas? Why is Japan so expensive, and India so cheap? And what should you do when you have failed (again) to communicate your plans for the evening to your partner? These essays demonstrate how economic ideas can provide unexpected illumination of familiar problems.

# Why does advertising contain so little information?

14 MARCH 1997

When I learnt economics, I was taught to take a dim view of advertising. In Economics 1, I had apples and you had pears. You wanted some apples and I wanted some pears, and that provided scope for beneficial exchange. A competitive market enabled each of us to trade apples and pears. That competitive market not only allowed exchange, but made sure it would be efficient.

So where did advertising come into this? It didn't. Shouting "eat apples" or "eat pears" created no more apples or pears, and indeed you had to feed apples and pears to the advertising agencies that did the shouting. And proclaiming "eat Bloggs' apples" or "eat Smith's pears" would, if successful, simply create market power and destroy the efficiency of a competitive market. Advertising was divided into the informative – apples are round and red and are available from greengrocers – and the persuasive – eat more apples.

The informative might be tolerated in modest quantity. The persuasive served no beneficial economic purpose. The standard text on the economics of advertising was a work by Lord Kaldor, economic guru of the last Labour government but one. Kaldor regarded advertising as a sinful activity which should be heavily taxed, like smoking, drinking, gambling, and employment in service industries.

And the advertising industry did not help itself much by the way it described itself. Be handsome in Levi's, seductive with Chanel, pull more birds in a Peugeot. Advertising seemed to appeal to essentially irrational instincts and less than admirable ones. The industry employed economists of doubtful virtue to argue that advertising helped secure scale economies and promoted economic growth. But if I didn't know I needed an aftershave, how am I better off when you both create and satisfy my unnecessary demand?

What you learn in an economics course today would be very different. A new subject has been created – the economics of information. A seminal article by George Akerlof described the market for lemons. Akerlof did not simply extend the apples and pears model to cover citrus fruit. Akerlof's lemon was a car made on a Friday afternoon in which nothing ever quite worked properly. (This was before the days when cars were made in Japan and just as good on Friday as on any other day of the week.) As a seller you knew whether or not your car was a lemon. The prospective purchaser did not.

Akerlof's achievement (for which he should get a prize some day), was to show that standard economic assumptions about market efficiency ceased to be valid in the face of differences in information. Lemons illustrated the problem well. Suppose 10% of all cars were lemons. You might expect the price of a second hand car to reflect the frequency of lemons in the overall car population. But if it did, then selling at that price would be attractive to the owners of lemons and unattractive to the owners of normal cars. So there would be a disproportionate number of lemons in the used car showrooms.

Realising this, buyers would reduce the price they were willing to pay. But the result is that only those with really dreadful cars, or those who are desperate for money, will put their cars on the market. The new price will not be low enough to reflect the original quality of the cars. In the end, there may be very little trade at very low prices. The market simply does not work.

One of the merits of Akerlof's analysis was that it met a test failed by too many economic models – consistency with common sense. After all, everyone knows that buying a used car is a depressing experience.

With the economics of information came a different view of the economic role of advertising. Modern economies include many activities, like selling cars, where product quality and product attributes are complex and sellers know far more about what they sell than buyers about what they buy. Advertising is about managing that gap in information. And when you look more closely at advertising with that perspective, you see that the

*Johnnie Walker whisky advertisement, 1906*

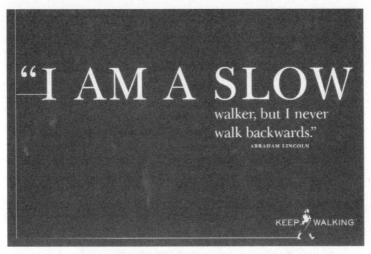

*Johnnie Walker whisky advertisement, 2001*

distinction between information and persuasion does not really
stand up.

Much advertising – indeed all of the most conspicuous and
costly advertising – was neither informative or persuasive. Early
twentieth century advertisements were full of positive statements
about the products they promoted. Johnnie Walker used to
advertise the merits of his company's whisky. In today's advertisement, you would not even realise what was being advertised if you
did not already know. Tobacco advertising demonstrates that you
can still advertise extensively – and presumably successfully –
when you are not allowed to make any claims for the product at
all, other than that it is bad for you.

So what is the purpose of such advertising? It was Richard
Nelson who noted that the only information it conveyed was that
the advertiser spent a lot of money on advertising. But, he argued,
this is useful information. It tells you that the advertiser is
committed to the product and the market. If he was not, it would
be absurd for him to spend so much. And if he is committed to the
product and the market, it also makes sense for him to devote

resources to ensuring the quality of his product.

So consumers are right to believe that branded products are of good quality, not because the manufacturer claims they are good quality – mostly they do not – but because there is little point in branding products that are not of good quality. And many of the products which are most heavily advertised are those for which Akerlof's information asymmetry is a problem – financial services, lavatory cleaners.

But not used cars. In that market, people don't buy often enough for commitment to the market to be proved worthwhile. The market for lemons is real.

---

George Akerlof did indeed win the Nobel Prize for economics in 2001 for his contributions to the economics of information, including the analysis set out in 'The Market for Lemons: Quality Uncertainty and the Market Mechanism' (1970) *Quarterly Journal of Economics*, 84, August, pp 488-500.

Nicholas Kaldor, whose 'Economic Aspects of Advertising' appeared in the *Review of Economic Studies* in 1950 became special adviser to the Chancellor of the Exchequer in 1964 and was in that capacity responsible for major reforms to the British tax system, including the introduction of Corporation Tax and Capital Gains Tax and, notoriously, Selective Employment Tax, a levy on employment in service industries. In 1974 he became Lord Kaldor. Richard Nelson's theory was put forward in 'Advertising as Information' (1973), *Journal of Political Economy*, 81, pp 729-754.

Johnnie Walker advertisements courtesy of Diageo plc.

# It's a small world

23 AUGUST 2000

A few years ago it was still possible to holiday in the troubled but beautiful province of Kashmir. I flew to Delhi, caught a smaller plane to Srinigar, and travelled on by jeep and boat. As a porter carried my bags up a dusty track to my destination, I encountered a friend from London. What a small world, we said.

But there was really no coincidence at all. If I had been dropped by helicopter at some random point on earth, and had met an acquaintance, that would have been an extraordinary event. There are six billion people in the world, and no-one can know more than a tiny fraction of them. But my arrival in Kashmir was not at all random. Travel agents in London deal with a small number of representatives in India, who deal in turn with a few providers in Kashmir. If my friend and I had expressed similar requests, it was not surprising we should end up at the same place. We were in closely connected networks.

Network externalities are a new buzzword in business economics. Connectedness is vital, and it is best to be connected to the largest network. Telephones are the archetype of the network externality. There is no point in being the only person with a telephone, and the more people with them the more valuable my phone becomes. Such network externalities give huge advantages to early, large, players. There are around two billion telephones in the world, and the company which has the highest proportion of this population signed up will attract most new subscribers.

There is one problem with this analysis. It is not how the telephone industry is organised. The world telephone system consists of many operators, large and small. Most provide service

9

in a particular geographical area, and connect each other's calls through negotiated access agreements. And, whatever large telcos may wish or say, the number of providers of telecommunications services is increasing.

Perhaps this happened because of government regulation of

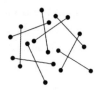

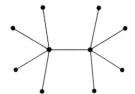

*Random connections*              *Clustered connections*

access and interconnection. But the banking industry evolved in just the same way without regulation. You open a current account because you want to make payments to other people. Most of the people to whom you want to make payments live in the same area. So early banks were local, and each bank made arrangements with banks in other towns and countries for the occasional transaction that needed these connections. Today, a network of clearing and correspondent agreements ensures that you can make a payment through your local bank to anyone in the world.

Suppose one bank – Silibank – decides that it will only make or accept payments from other Silibank accounts. If it signed up enough customers, then it would be able to exploit the network externality. Everyone would need a Silibank account, and it would become the dominant bank in the world. It would be a brilliant strategy if it succeeded. But there is not the slightest chance of it succeeding. All Silibank's customers would desert it for more flexible competitors.

Cash machines are another network, but one which does not require 'any to any' connectivity. You don't need access to every cash machine in the world, just to a reasonably large number. Yet cash machine networks function in just the same way as payment systems and telephones. There is some advantage to the bank with the most machines, but in practice negotiations between banks over interconnection ensure that all customers are served. These payment arrangements are the product of market forces, not regulation.

The same organisation is found in other network industries, such as gas and electricity distribution, or airlines. There are many operators, large and small, and they organise interchange and access. Although not universal these arrangements are general enough to allow the system to work as a network. And interconnectedness between competing providers is true of the most famous new network of all – the internet.

The model of network externalities – in which the company that is first to create the largest network denies access to competi-

---

## THE ORACLE OF BACON

### Ronald Reagan
was in *Hellcats of the Navy* (1957)
with Nancy Davis (Mrs Reagan)
who was in *You Can't Hurry Love* (1988)
with Bridget Fonda
who was in *Balto* (1995)
with **Kevin Bacon**

### Kevin Bacon
was in *Mystic River* (2003)
with Eli Wallach
who was in *Dream Factory* (1973)
with Gloria Swanson
who was in *Beyond the Rocks* (1922)
with **Rudolph Valentino**

tors and establishes an unassailable monopoly – is a theoretical possibility. But the only cases of it actually happening seem to be those in which governments have imposed it, as they did for national telephone services. Where evolution is left to market forces, the usual outcome is competition, interconnection and access.

And the phenomenon I discovered in Kashmir explains why. Graph theorists, who study networks, illustrate it through the Kevin Bacon hypothesis. Everyone who has ever been in a movie was in a movie with someone who was in a movie with someone who was in a movie with Kevin Bacon. Kevin Bacon is as much – and as little – the centre of the movie world as Gloria Swanson or the Fonda family.

Kevin Bacon, and our 'small world' experience show that overlapping clusters produce a very high degree of connectedness from a relatively modest number of direct links. That is why market forces ensure that network industries are organised that way. And why there is more than one agent in Hollywood, more than one bank, and why natural monopolies based on network externalities do not often exist.

---

The oracle of Bacon can be consulted at http://www.cs.virginia.edu/oracle/. Duncan Watts, *Small Worlds*, (1999) Princeton University Press and Mark Buchanan, *Ubiquity*, (2000) Weidenfeld & Nicolson, are general introductions to the properties of connected networks.

2 September 1998                                        Oxford

Dear Linda,
If you are reading this, Linda, I hope you still remember the evening
we spent together in Oxford thirty years ago. We dined at the
Elizabeth restaurant. We enjoyed the piperade, the suprême de
volaille, and the crème brulée, and much else.

   I had exactly the same meal there a few weeks ago. I have changed
and so, I expect, have you. But the Elizabeth has not. The décor is
just as it was, the service is still classically impeccable and the
piperade, the volaille and the crème brulée are still on the menu. The
coffee is brewed by the same vacuum process that brewed it then.

   But the price is very different. I don't have the bill for our dinner
(not even my Scottish canniness goes that far) but an old Good Food
Guide buried in the Bodleian Library tells me that I could have
bought that meal in 1968 for 31/- (or £1·55 as it became on decimal-
isation). This year, it cost me £23.

   Neither of us had ever then eaten a hamburger. McDonalds arrived
in the UK in 1974 and a Big Mac then cost 45p. Today you will pay
£1·84, an annual inflation rate of 6 per cent. These comparisons are
freaks. The curious time warp that envelopes the Elizabeth, and the
relentless standardisation of McDonalds, enable us to look at these
price changes with confidence that we are comparing like with like.
Most of the modern economy is not like that.

   If we had gone to Australia in 1960, we would probably have gone
by sea. A shared cabin on P&O would have cost us £132 each. Today
a standard single fare to Sydney is £791, a price rise of 5 per cent per
annum. But this is a very different product. I am willing to bet that
faced with the choice of a six week journey by sea for £132 or a

## THAT MENU

| 1968 | | 1998 |
|------|---|------|
| 6/6 | *Pipérade*<br>A basque dish of eggs with sweet<br>pimento and tomato | £6.50 |
| 19/6 | *Suprême du Volaille en Vin Blanc*<br>Breast of chicken in butter with<br>cognac, white wine and cream | £13.25 |
| 5/– | *Crème bruleé*<br>Custard cream with<br>caramelised topping | £4.00 |
| 31/– (1·55p) | | £23·75 |

twenty-four hour flight at £791, most people would choose Qantas. The improvement in quality more than offsets the increase in cost. When we recognise this, we see that the price of getting to Australia has not gone up. It has come down.

A brilliant essay by the American economist Bill Nordhaus provides a good illustration of the issues. Reported price indices measure changes in the price of light bulbs and of electricity. But we don't buy light bulbs because we want light bulbs. We buy light bulbs because we want light. Nordhaus showed that if you measure the price of light, rather than the price of the things you use to make light, the difference amounts to nearly 4% per year. The price of things for lighting has moved in line with general inflation: the price of light itself has fallen.

Health budgets around the world are under pressure from the escalating cost of medical services. But are these costs really rising? David Landes has recently explained how Nathan de Rothschild, probably then the richest man in the world, died prematurely in 1836 despite the best medical attention money could buy. He died from an

*infection which could today be cured by drugs available for a few pence
at any pharmacy. The cost of medicaments may have gone up, but the
cost – literally – of living has come down.*

*But these arguments do not all go one way. When I bought you
dinner, I was not really purchasing a suprême de volaille. I was
buying the best dinner Oxford could offer. To do that today, I would
have to take you to the Manoir aux Quat'Saisons, and pay the £72
that M. Blanc demands for a meal. That is equivalent to inflation of
16 per cent per annum. Fine dinners are a positional good – their
value rests on the fact that not everyone can afford them, and their
price rises with the incomes of the people who can afford them.*

*These problems are not minor quibbles. The developments I describe
– the creation of new, higher quality restaurants, the substitution of
new forms of transport for old, advances in medical technology, and
improvements in lighting efficiency – are typical of what has
happened right across the economy. And that is why the price indices
we use are hedged by doubts. As it happens, the cost of a meal at the
Elizabeth, rising at 11 per cent a year, almost exactly matches the
movement in the catering component of the Retail Prices Index. But I
could reduce catering inflation to 6 per cent by looking at the price of
a Big Mac or increase it to 16 per cent by measuring the change in the
cost of a very good evening out. You could present a good argument for
adopting any of these figures.*

*And if we are so uncertain about what has really happened to
prices, we are therefore uncertain about what has really happened to
output and economic growth. How do we compare a bundle of output
that consists of sea crossings, slide rules and Ealing comedies with one
made up of package holidays, computers and televisions? Only by
making a decision as to how many Ealing comedies equal one television. I don't know how to do that and nor does the Office for
National Statistics.*

*It is tempting to argue that we could solve these problems if we
were more careful in the way we compile economic statistics. There is
not much doubt that if we paid more attention to quality improvements*

and the consequences of the introduction of new goods the reported rate of inflation would be lower – probably much lower – and the reported rate of growth would be higher – probably much higher.

But the issue goes deeper. Am I better or worse off than Henry VIII? True, I have fewer wives, servants and palaces. But Henry suffered agonies from piles and could not get to Bristol in less than a week. Asking whether I would rather be me or Henry VIII is as stupid a question as asking whether I would be happier if I were a sheep or a fly, and the question is not made less stupid by dressing it up in figures. When someone tells you that inflation is 3·7 per cent and growth 2·1 per cent, be very wary of believing that these numbers tell you what has happened either to the cost or the standard of living.

John

The Elizabeth restaurant in Oxford finally closed in 2003, its dishes and rooms barely changed over four decades. The analysis by Bill Nordhaus is found in 'Do Real-Output and Real-Wage Measures Capture Reality?', in T. F. Bresnahan & R. J. Gordon (1997), *The Economics of New Goods*, Chicago University Press, and David Landes tells the story of Nathan Rothschild in his introduction to *The Wealth and Poverty of Nations*,(1998), Little, Brown. Positional goods were described by Fred Hirsch, *Social Limits & Growth*, (1976), (see p35)

# One day in Whitehall

16 SEPTEMBER 1998

FROM: Secretary of State
TO: Sir Humphrey Appleby
I was reading an article by John Kay in the car this morning. All about taking someone called Linda to the Elizabeth Restaurant in Oxford. He went on to suggest that official statistics were all wrong. Is there anything in it? It might have big implications for the way we run the economy. Anyway, anything that might unsettle Gordon Brown could come in handy.

FROM: Sir Humphrey Appleby
TO: Young High-flyer
Could you prepare a note on John Kay's article in the Financial Times?

FROM: Young High-flyer
TO: Sir Humphrey Appleby
John Kay's article is witty and incisive as usual. He argues that measurements of the cost of living fail to take adequate account of the introduction of new goods, substitution between goods, and quality improvements. For example, what the Office for National Statistics does is to track the rising price of candles till people switch to electric light, and then track the rising price of electricity. They miss the key point that electricity is so much more efficient than candles that artificial light, once a luxury for the rich, has become an affordable everyday commodity. Changes like these are happening everywhere. As a result, calculations of inflation are far more uncertain than we

acknowledge, and the inflation rate is probably overstated, perhaps substantially.

FROM: Sir Humphrey Appleby
TO: Young High-flyer
I am not sure you understood my memorandum. Have a look in the departmental manual, sub-section 174 (3)A(iii) part 17.

EXTRACT FROM DEPARTMENTAL MANUAL
The following format should generally be followed in response to external criticism of the department.
1. The points made in criticism of the department are incorrect.
2. The points made in criticism of the department are already being considered and changes in procedures are being made to respond to them. The suggestions made by the critic would delay this process and worsen the situation he describes.
3. The critic is evidently unaware that his suggestions have already been fully implemented by the department.
In the light of 1,2 and 3 above, the procedures of the department are wholly appropriate and no criticism of any member of it is warranted.

FROM: Young High-flyer
TO: Sir Humphrey Appleby
Is this better? See attachment.

FROM: Sir Humphrey Appleby
TO: The Financial Times, Secretary of State
Kay's article fails to acknowledge that the RPI is a measure of changes in the prices of a fixed basket of goods, and not of changes in the cost of living. In brief, the RPI is a measure of what it is the RPI measures, and is therefore entirely accurate. In any event,

considerable progress has been made in adjusting the RPI to take account of quality improvements, and changes of the kind proposed by Kay might lead to over compensation. Officials have long been aware of the problems noted by Kay and readers and ministers can be assured that the RPI fully reflects them. While the matter is constantly under review, whatever is being done at the moment is the best that could possibly be done.

FROM: Sir Humphrey Appleby
TO: Personnel
Young High-flyer is showing evidence of Permanent Secretary material. Mark his file accordingly.

FROM: DeAnne Dove
TO: Monetary Policy Committee
I am interested in this suggestion by John Kay that the official inflation rate may be overstated. If he is right, we may already have virtually stable prices. Wouldn't it then be time for an interest rate cut?

FROM: Governor, Bank of England
TO: Monetary Policy Committee
Steady! If it were established that the inflation rate were overstated, the Chancellor might wish to make a corresponding adjustment to the targets set for the Monetary Policy Committee. We need to consult the Treasury.

FROM: Permanent Secretary, Treasury
TO: Governor, Bank of England
In framing his inflation target, the Chancellor was influenced by two principal considerations: the benefits of price stability as such and concern that inflation tends to accelerate when it rises above a very low rate. While he would not wish to influence the deliber-ations of the Monetary Policy Committee in any way, he is sure

that these factors will be in the minds of the members of the Committee when they arrive at their independent judgement.

FROM: Deputy Governor
TO: Monetary Policy Committee
There is a useful article in the Bank of England Quarterly Bulletin (August 1997) quantifying the benefits of price stability. Broadly, the main advantages are the result of the lower interest rates which price stability brings about.

FROM: Director General, Confederation of British Industry
TO: Anyone who will listen
Isn't this a bit odd? If the main benefits of price stability are lower interest rates, why are we putting interest rates up to achieve price stability?

FROM: Henry Hawk, from Holland
TO: Monetary Policy Committee
Don't be deceived by the siren voices of the CBI. We have been putting interest rates up recently in order to avoid having to put them up by even more in future. Broadly, the Chancellor's two concerns reduce to one. Unless inflation is kept down to very low levels, it will spiral out of control.

FROM: John Kay
TO: Readers of the Financial Times
Perhaps this helps to confirm my suggestion. Any inflation tends to accelerate. The reason we feel safe with inflation of 2½% or so is that measured inflation of 2½% corresponds to virtual price stability if quality improvement is taken into account.

FROM: Deputy Governor
TO: Monetary Policy Committee
The effect of the two issues the Committee has been considering

is to offset each other. It may be that inflation has been overstated in the past. If this is the case, then the Chancellor should lower his inflation target correspondingly. Our views on what is a stable inflation rate are based on erroneous historic data. So if inflation continues to be overstated, we will come to the right decisions if we go on using the inflated figures. As the American economist Paul Krugman has put it, if you have got used to driving with a faulty speedometer, the best thing you can do is go on using it: you may drive worse, not better, if you have the speedometer fixed.

FROM: Sir Humphrey Appleby
TO: Secretary of State
Exactly, Minister.

FROM: Linda
TO: John Kay
Of course I remember that dinner in the Elizabeth Restaurant. It was the most boring evening of my life. You kept on talking about economics. Something to do with price indices and inflation, if I remember. It was only the prospect of the crème brulée that kept me sitting there till the end of the evening.

---

Sir Humphrey Appleby was the complacent civil servant who repeatedly outwitted his political master in Antony Jay's television series *Yes Minister*. DeAnne Julius (famously dovish) and the Dutch economist Willem Buiter (notoriously hawkish) were among the founding members of the Monetary Policy Committee of the Bank of England established in 1997 to determine British interest rates.

# A beautiful mind

30 SEPTEMBER 1998

Two star-crossed lovers – let us call them Linda and John – have a date this evening. But, once again, John has let the battery on his mobile phone go flat. They cannot talk to each other. What should they do?

John Nash, whose biography has just been published, is an American mathematician who devised a framework for thinking about such problems – the theory of non-co-operative games. Two or more agents make independent decisions and the outcome depends, for better or worse, on the interaction between them. That is the situation faced by Linda and John. Everyone engaged in business, politics, or everyday life plays non-co-operative games again and again.

John sits there thinking "what will Linda do"? And what she will do will depend, in turn, on what she thinks John will do. But what John will do depends, in turn, on what John thinks Linda thinks that John will do. And so on, for ever.

But suppose Linda and John share a favourite restaurant – the Elizabeth in Oxford, perhaps. Then Linda might think: suppose John were to be at the Elizabeth, what would be the best course of action for me? To go to the Elizabeth, of course. And the same is true for Linda. So even without a chat on the mobile phone, it would seem to make good sense for each to turn up at the Elizabeth at eight o'clock.

That happy coincidence cuts through endless rounds of speculation about the motives of others. Is there an outcome in which everyone is doing what is best for them, given the choices which have been made by everyone else? That is the definition of

a Nash equilibrium. If the concept seems rather obvious, it demonstrates that Nash's idea has one of the hallmarks of real scientific originality. It is obvious, once it has been pointed out to you. It wasn't before.

Still, there are problems to which the Nash solution is less trite than the recommendation to go to the Elizabeth at eight. Take the familiar business problem of how much capacity to build. The price you realise for your output depends on the total amount of capacity which everyone installs. This has a precise Nash equilibrium solution. The total amount of capacity which will be built increases with the number of firms which enter – but at a diminishing rate – and the amount of excess capacity will rise with the ratio of fixed to variable costs. We can write out the mathematics. And understand better why industries with higher fixed costs are prone to cyclical instability, and why they experience periods of acute price competition, and tend to be subject to cartels and to regular phases of rationalisation and consolidation.

But a Nash equilibrium need not be the actual outcome. Linda might get fed up and go home. John might have misunderstood what Linda said about the Elizabeth. And Linda and John could have found each other in many different Nash equilibria. If they want to be together sufficiently then meeting in Joe's greasy spoon café is another solution.

If there are many Nash equilibria, and there often are, then better ones should be preferred to worse. Still, it can happen the other way round. The QWERTY layout for keyboards is grossly inefficient. It was reportedly invented to slow users down in the days when typewriter keys were liable to jam. Other systems, like the Dvorak layout, are simpler and quicker to use. But if everyone else is using QWERTY, if most machines are made in QWERTY, the sensible thing to do is to learn and use QWERTY. And that is true for everyone else. Which is why we are stuck, for ever, with an inefficient Nash equilibrium. It is a demonstration of the power of the concept. Having reached a Nash equilibrium, we cannot leave it, even for a better one.

More confusing still are the cases where several Nash equilibria are equally good. Suppose John likes the Elizabeth but Linda prefers the Petit Blanc. If each follows their own preference, each will dine alone. But if Linda goes to the Elizabeth, she takes the risk that John, with equivalent altruism, will be at Le Petit Blanc – leaving them with the worse of all outcomes, in which they dine separately at their least preferred restaurants. The game is called the Battle of the Sexes by mathematicians, because it displays familiar features of personal relationships – lack of communication, confusion, and scope for the best of motives to be misunderstood.

But the Battle of the Sexes is actually the universal problem of co-ordination in business. It does not matter much what the outcome is, only that we should all pursue the same actions. The general answer to such coordination is hierarchy. If John's wishes are paramount, the outcome is likely to be better – not just for John, but for Linda. It does not really matter which side of the road we drive on, but it matters a great deal that everyone should drive on the same side of the road, and that is why it is necessary that someone should tell us what to do and that we should obey them.

Not an idea that goes down well in Oxford, or at Princeton, where Nash spent his career. That career – characterised by phases of outstanding originality broken by long bouts of paranoid schizophrenia – is a telling reminder that the originality and sensitivity associated with great insight may actually be disabling, not helpful, in everyday life. But we should not conclude that we cannot learn from these insights. Just as we need not admire Mozart's character to enjoy his music, or applaud Clinton's habits to benefit from his economic policies, we need not envy Nash's life to benefit from his ideas.

---

The biography of John Nash was Sylvia Nasar's *A Beautiful Mind*, (1998) Faber & Faber. In 2001 it was released as a film starring Russell Crowe as John Nash. Paul David's famous discussion of QWERTY is in 'Clio and the Economics of QWERTY' (1985) *American Economic Review*, 75 (2), May, pp 332-7 and the rule of the road is reviewed further on p 58.

# Everlasting light bulbs

I SEPTEMBER 1999

Last weekend, I bought some light bulbs for less than £2 each. The manufacturer claims they use one quarter of the electricity of a conventional light bulb and last ten times as long.

The story of the everlasting light bulb is one of the hoariest myths in business economics. According to legend, inventors have frequently come up with designs for an everlasting light bulb. These products would cost no more to make. But a conspiracy of light bulb manufacturers has always ensured that these innovations are suppressed, so that the continuing market for light bulbs is not spoiled.

As with all urban myths, there are numerous variations. The product is not always a light bulb. The same claims are made for tights: what woman would not rush to purchase a pair of long-lasting tights? Why don't batteries go on for ever? And then, it must surely be possible to build automobiles that would never wear out. But not only do Ford and General Motors choose not to do this: they constantly introduce superficial redesigns to their products to induce us to buy unnecessary replacements. We are all led to believe that built-in obsolescence is endemic to contemporary capitalism.

But the myth is indeed a myth. We do not need to appeal to the better nature, or environmental conscience, of light bulb manufacturers. They will not suppress the everlasting light bulb because it does not pay them to do so. The clearest demonstration of the issues was provided thirty years ago by an Australian economist, Peter Swan.

Suppose there are several competing producers of light bulbs.

Our hypothetical inventor approaches one of them. The firm will indeed recognise that ultimately, when all the world's bulbs have been replaced by the new discovery, its sales will fall. But until then, it will enjoy a hundred per cent market share. Most of the lost sales will be the lost sales of its competitors. Innovation has always been the mainstay of competition and no competitive firm would pass up such an opportunity.

Now give the story a more sinister turn. The myth relies on conspiracy. Even if an individual firm would seize avidly the opportunity created by the everlasting light bulb, the manufacturers would establish a cartel to see that our inventor was assassinated or otherwise removed from the scene.

But would they? Visualise yourself as the light bulb king, a John D. Rockefeller or Bill Gates striding above the world's light bulb industry. It is easiest to see how you would respond to the inventor if you imagine yourself renting rather than selling the services of your bulbs. And it is very likely that if you were a light bulb monopolist, this is what you would do. Renting out these prized objects would allow you to discriminate by reference to the ultimate use, charging more for office and public lighting than for domestic illumination. This is what utilities generally did when they had a monopoly. It is also how Xerox behaved so long as the company's patents over photocopiers remained effective. Rental gives you control: only once the photocopying market became competitive did sales take over from rental as the principal means of supply.

In such a world, the incentives of the light bulb monopoly are to charge whatever rental the market will bear, and to provide that service as cheaply as possible. The monopoly will grasp the benefits of the everlasting bulb for itself, and thank the inventor for adding to its profits. The rental structure makes the issue particularly clear, but there is no real difference if you monopolise the sale of light bulbs rather than the provision of light bulb services. You recoup the benefits of the new technology in the price of the bulb.

So a competitive firm would wish to introduce the everlasting light bulb as soon as possible, and so would a cartel or monopoly. It is a little harder, but still relatively straightforward, to deal with the cases in between perfect competition and true monopoly, and to show that the same arguments hold.

Built-in obsolescence arises mainly because consumers genuinely want new things. Trivially new brands of washing powder, or restyled automobile designs, or new season's fashions, are all the results of competition: they are the product of rivalry, not collusion.

And this account fits reasonably well with what has happened in the light bulb market. It was always possible to manufacture light bulbs that would last for many years. But the higher cost and lower efficiency of these bulbs meant that these were not in fact an attractive proposition for consumers. Only recently did new technology enable long life, low energy bulbs to be made at costs reasonably comparable to those of conventional bulbs.

And so long as the number of manufacturers of these new bulbs was relatively small, and production limited, their high prices took full account of their value to consumers. But as competition in the market increased, so price fell towards the cost of supply. Which is why I was able to buy my bulbs for £1.90. And the reason there are no eternal automobiles or indestructible tights is that at the price and in the quality at which these goods can be manufactured, they are not products many people wish to buy.

---

Peter Swan demolished the theory of the everlasting light bulb in 'The Durability of Consumption Goods', (1970) *American Economic Review*, 60, pp 884-94.

# The price of everything, the value of nothing

19 SEPTEMBER 1997

Adam Smith observed the paradox that water, which is essential to life, sells for almost nothing: while diamonds, almost useless, command a very high price. The explanation is that price depends on both supply and demand, and any analysis that does not look at both simultaneously goes badly wrong. Which explains why property and haircuts cost more in Beverley Hills and on the Côte d'Azur, where a lot of rich people live, but petrol and lycra leggings do not. And why garbage collectors earn a lot less than stockbrokers, even if their work is harder and probably more useful.

Yet the notion that things have an intrinsic value which is independent of their price remains a powerful one. And there is an economic term – consumer surplus – for the difference between the two. Consumer surplus is the difference between what you would be willing to pay for something – its price – and what you actually have to – its value.

For goods like water which are in plentiful supply, the consumer surplus may be very large. The average household water bill is around £2 per week: but what would you be willing to pay for water supply? You might grumble if the cost went up to £10 per week. But suppose I came to turn your water supply off. Think of going down to the Thames every morning to get the washing water. Think of boiling it before you peeled the vegetables or prepared the salad. £50 per week starts to seem reasonable. That makes the consumer surplus you get from water at least twenty times what you actually have to pay.

And yet not all the water you use yields much consumer surplus. Most of it actually goes into low value uses – watering the garden, washing the car. As Figure 1 shows, the total consumer surplus – the triangle – is the sum of the consumer surplus you get from each litre: from the very large amount from the first sip of water you drink to the negligible amount from the water that is barely worth to you what it costs.

Turning consumer surplus into profit is a central business objective. For water, this is such an easy opportunity that we have an Office of Water Services whose primary job is to stop it happening. There is no such agency in the diamond market; just the opposite. Consumer surplus is smaller anyway, precisely because diamonds are not as useful as water and there are not so many of them around. But it is also smaller because much of the potential consumer surplus has been grabbed by de Beers in the course of its century old control of the world diamond market.

de Beers has split the consumer surplus triangle into three parts by pushing price above the cost of supply. The rectangle in figure 2 is the company's profit. The upper triangle is the consumer surplus that remains. The triangle on the right measures the consumer surplus that customers have lost but de Beers have not gained – it represents people who would like to buy diamonds for more than they cost but less than the company charges.

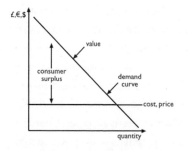

*Figure 1: Consumer surplus*

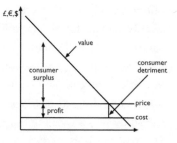

*Figure 2: Extracting value*

So how do you get hold of more of the upper triangle, and reduce the size of the lower? Figure 2 shows the most you can get if you are obliged to sell at the same price to everyone and for every unit. There are ways to do better. One is to sell at different prices to different people. Airlines sell the same essential product for very different revenues to first, business and economy travellers, and often segment the market far beyond that. Publishers sell first in hardback to libraries and aficionados, and later in paper at lower prices to a mass market. The manufacturers of new gismos, like video recorders or digital cameras, pick off the enthusiasts first and then sell at progressively lower prices to less interested buyers.

Another route is to sell goods as packages. de Beers does this through its famous system of sights, in which jewels are sold only as collections and buyers are not allowed to pick and choose. Selling a package makes sense only if the customer's decision to buy one part of the package means that he or she will pay less than other people for the second. There is no reason to sell instant coffee and Kit-Kat together simply because both are made by Nestlé unless coffee drinkers are particularly averse to Kit-Kat, or Kit-Kat munchers are only willing to pay low prices for their Nescafé. This is unlikely.

But if you buy a lot of water, then the extra you want is for your garden or your swimming pool; so water companies could (and would if they were allowed to) extract lots of consumer surplus by offering tariffs which decrease with the amount you use. If you are already paying for several television channels, then you do not have the same willingness to pay for more, because there are only so many hours in the day you can spend watching television. So Sky Television can (and is allowed to) extract plenty of consumer surplus by selling its channels, like de Beers diamonds, in bundles.

And there is a warning there for water companies, de Beers and Sky. You can only extract consumer surplus so long as you have market power. In competitive markets, consumer surplus all goes to the customers. Which is what differentiates petrol and lycra from property and hairdressing.

---

The principle that consumer surplus goes to customers when markets are competitive is one that was widely forgotten in valuing technology stocks after 1997.

# Guess who's come to dinner?

24 APRIL 2003

DINNER PARTY BORE: The people next door have just sold their house. Ours must be worth at least twice what we paid for it!

DINNER PARTY HOST: Only twice what you paid for it! We could sell ours, buy a mansion in Cornwall, and still have enough to cruise round the world five times.

ANOTHER BORING GUEST: But prices are bound to crash. Everyone says so.

FORMER CITY ECONOMIST, NOW EMPLOYED AS WAITER: If you don't mind my interrupting, I wouldn't believe anything commentators say. They don't know. And even if they did, they aren't disinterested – they want you to buy, or sell, or just want to attract your attention. People who predict house prices are no more credible than people who predict share prices. Believe me, I used to be in the prediction business.

GUEST: But the ratio of house prices to household incomes is at an all time high!

ECONOMIST: There is a mistaken analogy here between the price-earnings ratio for houses and the price-earnings ratio for shares. The stock market multiple usually reverts to its long run trend. That's why – I realise now – shares were overvalued in 2000.

GUEST: That would have been useful to know! But surely people can't spend an ever increasing proportion of their incomes on housing, any more than they can spend an ever increasing proportion of their incomes buying pet food on the internet.

ECONOMIST: That's insightful: if I'd understood it earlier, I might still have a job. You are right to focus on the costs of house ownership rather than the cost of houses. Interest rates have fallen so much that a typical mortgage payment is lower than it was ten years ago.

HOST: So you think prices could rise further! Perhaps we could buy a château on the Loire as well as a mansion in Cornwall, darling.

ECONOMIST: Not so fast! Interest rates were high when inflation was high, so even if the initial cost of a mortgage seemed crippling, people could expect the burden to become easier. And mortgage repayments are only a small part of the cost of buying a house: you have to pay for repairs and maintenance, heat and light, property taxes.

HOST: So the people in your old firm who used to get huge bonuses must be feeling the pinch.

ECONOMIST: Some of them are. The economist Fred Hirsch wrote about positional goods – commodities in limited supply would always be owned by the richest people. Trophy wives, for example, like your lovely spouse. Houses are the archetypal positional good. Competition for them means that the distribution of house prices will more or less reflect the distribution of incomes. With increasing income inequality over the last twenty years, prices of the most desirable houses have risen faster than those of simple homes. That trend could easily be reversed.

HOST: Maybe you'd better start looking for our country property right away, my dear! But why are Cornish house prices so much lower ?

ECONOMIST: Supply and demand. Land near capital cities is scarce, so its price is correspondingly high. And population has moved from rural to urban areas. The value of your Cornish mansion will be less than its rebuilding cost. If it didn't already exist, no one would build such a property now.

GUEST: So you think this talk of a house price bubble is overdone?

ECONOMIST: Somewhat. In classic bubbles – from tulip mania to the dot.com frenzy – people bought things, not for their intrinsic worth, but to sell on to others at a higher price. That rarely happens with houses.

GUEST: So why does the housing market keep having booms and busts?

ECONOMIST: Because of tittle tattle like this. When people think that prices will rise, they jump into the market: if they fear prices may fall, they are quicker to sell. As in every asset market, short term price movements are driven by beliefs, not underlying realities.

GUEST: So what do you really think is going to happen?

ECONOMIST: I used to say on the one hand, then on the other hand, but now only when I'm doing silver service. Short term expectations of a price fall will probably be self-validating. But who knows what will happen in the long run. The one thing I can tell you is the people who pontificate about these things don't know any more about them than you.

HOST: And that's why it's time for you to use both hands for the washing up.

---

*Social Limits to Growth*, by Fred Hirsch, was published by Routledge in 1977.

# Where do economists go on holiday?

27 AUGUST 2002

I'm looking at the postcards on the mantelpiece. Perhaps it's because the senders know I'm an economist. They mostly make the inevitable comments about the weather and go on to remark about the prices. You can learn a lot of economics if you keep your eyes open on holiday.

There is one from a pair of students, backpacking in India. They're amazed at how cheap it is. But that's why they go; if you can find accommodation for $10 a night then a few weeks of work will pay for an extended holiday. But in India even luxury hotels are cheap by European standards.

Japan is another matter altogether. The only way to enjoy touring there is to forget about currency conversions. If you start, you'll want to go straight back to Narita airport.

Purchasing power parity is fundamental to exchange rate economics. On a day-to-day basis, currencies are very volatile. But over an extended period, relative rates of inflation in different countries are by far the best predictor of exchange rate movements. Yet purchasing power parity implies that the cost of living will be the same everywhere. And every returning holiday-maker knows that isn't true.

The cost of living is generally higher in rich countries than poor ones. Prices in Norway are very high, but Norwegians can afford it. Or so one of my postcards says. But a full explana-tion is more complicated. Purchasing power parity means that prices of tradeable goods – such as clothes, cars and confectionery – tend to equalise around the world. The price of services varies much more, in line with the cost of domestic labour. And

these costs are higher in countries such as Norway.

The result is that rich countries tend to have higher exchange rates than would seem justified by purchasing power parity, and poor countries tend to have lower ones. If you look at the dispersion of standards of living across the world, it is much less than the dispersion of output per head calculated at market exchange rates.

Tourist expenditures contain a much higher proportion of services than day-to-day living. When you are at home, mostly you make your own bed, pour your own tea and mow your own garden. But when you travel, other people do these things for you. So the tourist cost of living shows even greater divergences than the residential cost of living.

This explains why India is a good destination for backpackers. But it doesn't explain why even Americans and Europeans find Japan so expensive, since income levels in their home countries are much the same. Japanese productivity in manufactured goods

– which enter into international trade – is high relative to Japanese productivity in services, which mostly aren't traded. So the price of services relative to goods is much higher in Japan than in Europe or the US.

The Japanese see this as a difference in quality. Not even the most expensive US hotels employ someone to bow as you enter or leave the lifts, while cooks in a steak house do not require the skills of a *keiseki* chef. What is meant by quality is intrinsically subjective. When in Rome, the prices you face will reflect Roman tastes, not your own. Purchasing power parity is too crude to cope with these cultural differences. It may equalise the wholesale price of manufactured goods, but when you buy these goods in a shop you also have to pay the price of local retailing services. That's why a Japanese camera may cost you more in Tokyo than it would in New York.

The camera is also expensive because the price of land, like the price of services, doesn't equalise internationally. Values are highest in the most congested parts of the world, such as London and Paris, Ginza and Manhattan, Hong Kong and Monaco. Property values don't only influence what you pay for an apartment or a hotel room. They affect the price of other goods you buy that use property – a cinema seat or a drink in a bar.

Property is cheaper where there are wide open spaces, as in Australia or the US. That is why these countries have a higher standard of living than would seem to be justified by their output. Property is also cheaper where there is no single dominant city. There are few prices in Spain, Italy or Germany that match those of London, Paris, or Tokyo. And property is cheap where there has been outward migration of population, because the stock of houses exceeds the demand. A French chateau is as cheap as an English country cottage because English agricultural decline happened so much earlier. And you can buy a Georgian house in Yorkshire or Northumberland for the price of a flat in the English home counties.

So where do economists go for holidays? Some of them frequent business hotels when businesspeople are no longer on business. They respond to the advertisements that offer bargain stays in Düsseldorf in August. They look for countries with low incomes per head, in which services will be cheap. They seek out countries with lower productivity in manufacturing goods than in services. They enjoy empty spaces, not for their environmental attributes, but for the low prices. And keep an eye out for the places where the population is moving out rather than moving in. Perhaps eastern Europe is the place to be. But there is more to life than economics. That's why this article was written in the south of France.

# The global economy

The dominant themes of popular discussion of business and economics in the 1990s were globalisation and technology.

For Tom Friedman, who chronicled globalisation for the *New York Times*, the process was 'as inevitable as the dawn'. Business people, bankers, consultants and international agencies applauded it. But demonstrators threw stones at them, and burnt down branches of McDonalds.

The global marketplace was associated with the new economy. Technology, it was claimed, changed fundamentally the traditional rules of economic engagement. The most immediate consequence was an extraordinary bubble in stock prices, centred on, but by no means confined to, businesses associated with the internet.

The essays here explore different aspects of globalisation and new technology, with an emphasis on the historic context and evolution. Both history and geography still make a big difference.

# The case for globalisation

25 JULY 2001

Any decent, thoughtful person is upset by conditions in factories in poor countries – and by the knowledge that many such factories are run by western firms that supply the goods we buy in our western shops. Typically, workers in them put in far longer hours than we could manage. They do jobs that are at best repetitive and are often far worse. They live and work in an environment that we would find intolerable. They do all this for very little money.

Many of the Genoa protesters are malevolent individuals for whom one excuse to throw Molotov cocktails is as good as any other. But their activities are possible because they have found a cause which attracts the support of many well-meaning people. Modern states can take vigorous actions against organized crime, but are vulnerable to terrorism if the professed objects of the terrorists are shared by many who would not themselves engage in terrorism.

At London's May Day demonstration, two bicycling demonstrators carried a placard demanding that 'capitalism should be replaced by something nicer'. It captures exactly the incoherence of anti-capitalists in the post-socialist world. But who does not sympathize with the thought?

Perhaps poor countries would have been better off without globalisation – without modern technology and without exposure to modern consumer goods, and without knowledge of the extraordinary material standards of living which have been achieved in western economies. That view involves a misty-eyed view of the idylls of peasant life. It is held mostly by those whose own everyday experiences are very different. The argument that we were happier when ignorant of other countries should be dismissed, not because it is necessarily wrong, but because it is no longer relevant.

Countries which have tried more recently to reject outside influences – like Burma, Cambodia, and Afghanistan – are countries with the most unpleasantly repressive regimes anywhere. They have to be, to maintain ideological zeal in the face of the impossibility of their policies, and to continue to suppress the aspirations of most of their citizens.

It is not feasible to pretend the modern economic world does not exist. But it certainly is feasible for both developed countries and poor countries to restrict the impact of globalisation by limiting trade and investment between them. The economist's usual answer is that this would make both the rich and the poor worse off. After all, unpleasant though working conditions are in Indonesian sweatshops, people choose to work there in preference to the grinding poverty that otherwise awaits them.

There is some truth in that: but we should not be too sanguine about it. The decisions of semi-literate thirteen year olds are not necessarily the choices of rational economic men and women. Family pressures and naive dreams of wealth lead people to take jobs in the market economy. Still, the blunt fact of economic history – the experience of Britain's industrial revolution, the background to emigration to the United States, and the reality of modern shanty towns – is that wherever industrial jobs have become available, people have left the land in large numbers to take them. And that makes it hard to argue that we would make these people better off by denying them the opportunity.

But isn't this only because the alternatives available in poor countries are so bad? That may be true, but what does it imply we should do? The depressing conclusion of fifty years of aid projects is that there is not much to show for them. Not enough to suggest that the distribution of world income would be very different if aid packages had been much larger. The development models of South Korea and Taiwan are not particularly admirable. Their extraordinary growth happened under despotic governments, through corrupt and nepotistic business sectors, and transformed rural environments into grubby industrial landscapes. And, although most of the population of these states is now materially much better off, they demonstrate gross inequalities of income and wealth.

One would like there to be nicer models of economic development. But there do not seem to be any. The governments of South Korea and Taiwan have been content to allow their citizens to be victims of globalisation. And, taken as a whole, they have not done badly out of it.

Could we allow western firms to operate in poor countries, but require them to operate to western standards of conditions and wages? This is tantamount to stopping them from operating at all (as the trade unionists who advocate such policies well know). And the effects of establishing rich enclaves in poor societies would be equivocal. Almost nothing is so destabilizing and debilitating, both economically and politically, as the immediate juxtaposition of rich and poor. You see that when pursued by beggars as a tourist in a poor country, or in the illegal traffic in people from eastern Europe or across the Rio Grande.

The best we can do in a hugely imperfect world is to encourage western firms to operate in poor countries, and require them to operate, not to the standards we would ourselves expect, but to the best standards that exist locally. And use our economic pressure as consumers and our political pressure as voters to impose our will.

We should also honestly debate the problems and opportunities of economic development. The opponents of globalisation cannot be defeated by steel fences or by lectures on the theme that you cannot buck the market. If capitalism's presentation of itself is so hectoring and unappealing that only economists, investment bankers and well-paid executives subscribe to it, public opinion will buck the market however uncomfortable the results may be for everyone concerned.

---

The G8 economic summit was held in Genoa in July 2001 with the Italian Prime Minister, Silvio Berlusconi, as host. A steel fence was built to protect the delegates from demonstrations. But the very intensity of the security precautions, and the billionaire Berlusconi's own reputation for dubious business dealings, attracted more vigorous protest than had been seen at any other economic meeting.

2 *February 2000*                                              *Davos*

*Dear Linda,*

*Greetings from Davos. I am basking in the sun on the terrace of the Schatzalp, the alpine meadow which overlooks the conference centre. The Americans are in town. Bill Clinton and his entourage have just passed through.*

*The hotels are filled with missionaries of the New Economy, and every session with an 'e' in the title is full to overflowing. Larry Summers, the US Treasury Secretary, has been here to explain the American miracle. If we would only listen and follow, we too could enjoy high productivity, low inflation, and falling unemployment. Christian Sautter, the French finance minister, looked sheepish as he shared the platform with Mr Summers, and assured his audience that France.com was on its way. Most of the transatlantic visitors are too polite to address their patronising messages directly to their Swiss hosts.*

*But when the International Monetary Fund came to Switzerland last year its officials showed no similar restraint. The Swiss were no doubt gratified that the IMF "commended the authorities for their successful macroeconomic management that had contributed to Switzerland's improved economic performance since 1997". However this encouragement was only to mitigate the agency's strictures on what had gone before. "The long recession during the first half of the 1990's came on the heels of an already sub-par long run GDP growth performance since the mid 1970's." The IMF went on to prescribe the now familiar nostrums: "Directors emphasised the need for more vigorous implementation of structural reforms to improve Switzerland's long-term growth performance".*

*But when I used the advanced technology available at Davos to*

THERE WAS A MARKED UPTURN IN LEADING ECONOMIC INDICATORS TODAY AS ECONOMISTS STOPPED FIDDLING WITH THE ECONOMY AND WENT TO DAVOS

ROGER BEALE

*look up the facts, it did not seem that the Swiss have anything to apologise for. When the World Economic Forum first met in 1970, output per head in the United States was almost 50% higher than the figure for Switzerland, converted to US dollars; the same comparison in 1999 shows Switzerland 15% ahead. Last year Alan Greenspan, chairman of the US Federal Reserve, gave the United States the twin blessings of low inflation and low unemployment. But the Swiss National Bank delivered even lower inflation and even lower unemployment than the Fed. As it has done in 24 of the 30 years that the World Economic Forum has assembled. When I recounted this to an American visitor in one of the Davos taverns, he complained loudly about the price of his cup of coffee. And he had a point.*

*The high cost of property and services in Switzerland means that the real incomes of the Swiss are not as high as their productivity would suggest. On the other hand, Switzerland has large and increasing foreign assets, while the United States has large and* increasing foreign debts. And Switzerland seems to do pretty well on those components of the standard of living that the national income statistics don't pick up.

There are parts of the United States as beautiful as the surroundings of Davos, but they are not the parts of the United States in which most of the population lives. That is one of the reasons why Klaus Schwab finds it easy to attract so many American visitors here. Most Swiss enjoy an aspect over clean lakes and clear mountains, and have ready access to an enviable transport network and state school system.

If you focus on living standards rather than productivity, the story is less marked but essentially the same. There was once a gap between Switzerland and the United States but Switzerland has caught up.

How are these economic statistics to be reconciled? If Switzerland has experienced slower growth than the United States over the last thirty years – and the IMF correctly reports the Swiss government's own figures – how can it be that Switzerland's economy has overtaken that of the United States in precisely the same time frame?

The answer to this question is interesting and unexpected. One of the claims of the New Economy geeks is that conventional measures of economic growth don't 'get it'. We fail to record properly the impact of new technology in creating new goods and improving the quality of old ones. And there does seem to be evidence that this is true – for Switzerland. Whatever Harry Lime may have thought, Switzerland no longer rotates with the cuckoo clock.

While tourism and financial services remain important, the modern Swiss economy is based on speciality chemicals and precision machinery. These account for about 60% of Swiss exports and almost a quarter of total output. The value of these sales in global markets has increased very rapidly since 1970. The variety and quality of Swiss goods – measured by the acid test of what international customers are willing to pay – has been steadily improving. And the output statistics to which the IMF refer essentially omit this improvement in the terms of trade. The price insensitive demand for

*technology-based Swiss products explains why Switzerland, unlike*
*the United States, runs a large trade surplus. And why the value of*
*Swiss output, and the real incomes of Swiss people, have moved*
*ahead of the United States.*

*The New Economy is here, in the canton of Graubunden. Not only*
*in the seminar rooms of the Davos Congress Centre. But in the*
*factories the Forum participants barely noticed as their limousines*
*sped by on the way from Zurich airport. In these businesses the*
*knowledge economy is already being incorporated into products for*
*which there are paying customers.*

*John*

---

The World Economic Forum, held in the pretty Swiss mountain resort of
Davos was founded by Klaus Schwab and is widely regarded as the most
prestigious of economics and business conferences. Its meeting in February
2000 represented the final climax of the 'new economy' mania and associated stock market bubble.

# An Economist's Tale:
## Everybody's gone surfin'

19 APRIL 2000

Once upon a time, Uncle Sam had a good idea. Or, to be more accurate, his niece and nephew, Dot and Com, had a good idea. Dot and Com lived in California and spent most of the day surfing. Uncle Sam found it difficult to understand exactly what the good idea was: but he knew that Dot and Com were very clever, he admired Dot's long legs and Com's tan and their enthusiasm convinced him that their good idea would succeed.

So Uncle Sam went to see his banker, Mr M. Old Mr M had seen many enterprises come, and almost as many go. That had made him cynical, but also rich. Uncle Sam knew that Mr M would back the venture, because of his long and profitable relationship with Uncle Sam. In turn, Mr M would expect Dot and Com to live frugally and work every hour of the day for several years, until the business turned into profit, and perhaps even until it started to generate cash.

But old Mr M was buried beneath his last tombstone, and young Mr M had taken his place. Uncle Sam knew immediately that young Mr M was very different. Old Mr M had never been known to remove his jacket (not even, Uncle Sam suspected, when he went to bed.) Young Mr M's red braces were visible for all to see.

Banking was not as it had been, young Mr M explained. In the old days, new industries had needed large capital investments. The patriarchs whose portraits were on the wall of Mr M's office had raised money for railroads and electric utilities. They had built

Mr M's office then

Mr M's office now

automobile plants and funded oil wells and airlines.

But today, Mr M explained, we live in a weightless economy. Knowledge based businesses don't require large capital investments. They need money to pay salaries and consultancy fees while the good ideas fructify. They also need to cover their large advertising and public relations expenses. Everyone could see what railroads and automobiles were for, but good ideas today seem to require a lot more explanation. Still, these expenditures hardly compare with the costs of a steelworks or a gas pipeline.

Uncle Sam sympathised with young Mr M. He had been made redundant once or twice himself, and he knew what it felt like. What was Mr M planning to do, Uncle Sam asked, now that fledgling companies didn't need bankers any more? Young Mr M laughed. Although there was no paper on his desk, there were many paperweights. He explained that his firm had raised more money for new businesses in the last year than in the whole of old Mr M's lifetime. Uncle Sam was puzzled. If these knowledge businesses didn't need large scale investment, why was Mr M raising capital for them, and where was the money going?

Mr M laughed again. Poor old Uncle Sam just didn't get it. Modern investment banking wasn't about funding capital projects. It was about spotting entrepreneurship. Bright young people like Dot and Com deserved to be rewarded for their good ideas. Their friends should be rewarded for knowing them, and for introducing them to Mr M. And their advisers, like Mr M's private equity division and Mr M himself, should also have a share of the action.

Mr M tapped a few numbers into his computer. If Dot and Com's idea was as good as Uncle Sam said, then it was worth.... he named a figure that took Uncle Sam's breath away.

By now, Uncle Sam was beginning to understand. He was just very old-fashioned in thinking that banks and stock exchanges were there to finance investment. The purpose of modern capital markets was to give young people immediate access to the money their good ideas would produce in future. He started to think of the things that Dot and Com would be able to buy. Nice houses, celebrations on the beach. He hoped he could join some of them. Uncle Sam had thought he would give Dot and Com a helping

*Surfin' USA*

hand. But now he realised that they would soon be helping him.

The values of the new economy were very different from those Uncle Sam remembered sharing with old Mr M. Fine residences and grand parties used to be things that came after your business had succeeded, not before. Another of old Mr M's maxims was that a bird in the hand was worth two in the bush. Young Mr M calculated the net present value of the flock before the first egg had hatched.

Times had indeed changed, Uncle Sam reflected, as he took the subway home. But one of Mr M's answers still troubled him. Uncle Sam now understood where the capital being raised went. But where had it come from?

Mr M had explained that there were two parts to the answer. Some of the money was derived from Uncle Sam's pension fund. Uncle Sam's trustees were putting his annual contributions into these start-ups, and even ditching shares in old Mr M's businesses to find more cash for talented girls and boys like Dot and Com. Uncle Sam had always thought that pension funds were there to help old people supplement their incomes at the end of their working lives, not to help young people supplement their incomes at the beginning of their working lives, but he supposed that just showed how out of date his thinking was.

And net investment in the US stock market had been associated with a fall in savings and an increase in borrowings, largely from abroad. After all, since these good ideas were going to make everyone much richer in future, there was no need to put money aside in the time-honoured way.

What would happen, Uncle Sam wondered, if Dot and Com's good idea wasn't as good as he and Mr M both thought it was? Who would pay his pension, and repay the foreign borrowings? Not to worry, he reflected. Dot and Com were good kids and he had a lot of confidence in them. A tear ran down his cheek. Uncle Sam had finally got it.

---

The Nasdaq index, dominated by high technology stocks, reached an all time peak of 5132 on 10 March 2000.

# Crying for Argentina

16 JANUARY 2002

Argentina, stumbling through yet another crisis, is the world's most unsuccessful economy. There are many countries poorer. But Argentina is a poor country that was once rich.

A century ago, standards of living in Argentina were not very different from those of western Europe. You can see that if you visit the older parts of Buenos Aires. They have all the elegance of European capital cities of the same period. Today, output per head in the big European economies is four or five times as great.

An even more relevant comparison is with other countries that were populated by European immigrants – Australia, Canada, New Zealand and the United States. Those who went to Argentina were mostly Spaniards and Italians, while the English-

speaking settlements were mainly populated by northern Europeans. But there were few other differences. In economic terms, Argentina was as much a British colony as Australia, with which it is often compared. Many readers' grandparents will have bought Argentine bonds or stock in Buenos Aires tramways.

What was it that went right for Australia and wrong for Argentina? An empty country can assign land rights in one of two ways. (The settlements were not empty, but the settlers behaved as if they were). Rights can be allocated from the top down – the government distributes or sells the land. Or they can be allocated from the bottom up – the government recognises the land claims of those who are first to settle on it. Every newly settled country has experienced tension between these two mechanisms.

The history of the debate is best documented for the United States. The American revolution ended the fiction that continues even today in Britain – all rights in land derive from the Crown. Even before they had framed their constitution, the victorious colonists approved the Northwest Ordinance, which assigned rights in unsettled land to the Federal Government.

But the federal government was often thousands of miles away from the action. When it tried to enforce its authority on the people who occupied land, the squatters mostly won. And, in a democratic society, squatters acquired increasing political influence as well. The main success of the Federal government in land allocation was in assigning small plots to war veterans. The Civil War, which removed the influence of large southern landowners and created an even larger class of veterans, settled the issue. The Homestead Act of 1862 allowed anyone who settled and cultivated a 160 acre plot of land to claim it as his own.

In Argentina – and in other Spanish speaking settlements such as Chile – the argument was resolved the other way. Central government succeeded in distributing land to the rich and influential. The beneficiaries were not good landowners, in the main: like many large landowners, they preferred the bright lights of capital cities to close involvement with the sources of their wealth. And, more important, the unequal distribution of income and wealth that resulted never enjoyed popular legitimacy.

So Argentine politics has been polarised for well over a century between the haves, who need to maintain control of the state in order to maintain their privileges, and the have-nots, who see these same privileges as the cause of their own poverty. And power has alternated between military dictators defending the status quo and populists like Juan Peron. Argentine politics is the source of Argentina's modern economic problem: but its historic economic problem is the source of its politics.

Today, as always, Argentina looks externally to explain its failure. The best known Argentine economist is Raoul Prebisch, who developed dependency theory: the idea that geographically peripheral economies, forced to subordinate their interests to the controlling influence of western Europe, were fated to inevitable decline. And, more recently, subordinated to the domination of the United States: although the history of the United States shows how a peripheral economy can actually outpace the centre. The success of Australia and Canada makes the same point. The Argentine response was different: in response to dependency theory, Argentina imposed trade barriers and embarked on extravagant projects of domestic industrialisation, with the same lack of success that these policies enjoyed everywhere else.

There will be no new frontiers. Yet post-Communist Russia encountered a very similar issue. Its equivalent of empty land was the complex of state-owned industry and mineral resources. Applying the theory that as long as private ownership was created it did not matter whose private ownership it was, many of these assets were allowed to fall into the hands of the rich and influential. The results were similar to those in Argentina. The new owners are more concerned to exploit their assets than to develop them. And the lack of legitimacy of the structure of property rights creates – as in Argentina – a polarisation between those who must maintain political influence to protect their economic interests and those who see no benefit to themselves from the current economic system.

The depressing lesson of Argentina is that this is a trap from which it has never been possible to escape. Let us hope that Russia fares better.

_____

Hernando de Soto's book *The Mystery of Capital,* (2000), Bantam Press, explores the evolution of land ownership in different countries with a particular discussion of the US experience.

# Why do foreigners drive on the wrong side of the road?

7 AUGUST 2003

This question baffles every Englishman abroad. The French, Chinese and Americans, who insist on driving on the right, greatly outnumber the British, Indian and Japanese who know that you should drive on the left.

Some explanations are intriguing, but wrong. Such as the claim that American and French revolutionaries switched to the right to snub George III and the Pope, and demonstrate the triumph of democratic rationality over established order. The French stuck to the right even before the fall of the Bastille, and the rule of the road was not an issue in the American War of Independence.

There are romantic but implausible myths: English knights and Japanese samurai, mostly right-handed, kept to the left to facilitate drawing their swords on the approaching enemy. The Arthurian tradition may still influence English life, but not that much. More banal accounts are perhaps better founded: the design of carriages made different habits more appropriate in different areas of the world.

This search for explanation misses the central point. The rule of the road is an extreme example of a compatibility standard. It does not matter what we do so long as we all do the same thing. There need be no underlying explanation. Chance events have extensive consequences. That gives us the famous metaphor of the butterfly whose flapping wings set off a tornado thousands of miles away. But we learn very little by tracking down the guilty butterfly. Our objective should be to understand the process of development, not to identify the chance event that created it.

The rule of the road has evolved under the influence of two factors which determine not only how we drive, but much of the world in which we live. The rule is the product of cultural and economic imperialism, mediated by the spread of habits of behaviour amongst geographically contiguous populations. Most leftist countries, other than Japan, are former British colonies and British railway engineers took leftism on the tracks around the world. But although their trains may be different, most former French countries drive on the right. Korea moved to the right when the Japanese were expelled. The German and Argentine invaders of the Channel and Falkland Islands switched these territories to the right, and the islanders celebrated their liberation by switching back. Leftism waxed and waned with the British empire.

Where competing standards are juxtaposed, the larger and more powerful area tends to win out. Canadians drove on the left in British Columbia and in the traditionally English maritime provinces: but in the centre of the country, where French and American influence was greater, the rule was to stay to the right. The construction of trans-Canadian highways made this untenable and in the 1920s Canada standardised – on the right.

In Europe, the right – long the practice of France and Spain – eventually became universal. Sweden was the last continental European country to fall in line, in 1967. Almost all the countries which have made a switch since the end of the First World War – about thirty in all – have moved to the right. But as road networks become more complex and street furniture becomes more extensive, the costs of changeover have steadily increased. Britain and Japan are likely to remain leftist islands in a rightist world.

But what of the United States? Why did the most successful of Britain's former colonies not follow the lead of its colonial master? Settlement and independence came too early for British influence to be decisive. There was not enough transport before 1750 for the rule of the road to have much significance, but in

*No entente cordiale*

countries going through the industrial revolution there was sufficient traffic by 1850 for a rule to be necessary. The United States was free to go its own way in that critical hundred years, and did.

The wings of the butterfly flap first one way, then another. General James Wolfe took Quebec, and in consequence North America speaks English, not French. The French lost the language war. But most of the world drives on the right, as on the Champs Elysée.

---

Path dependency – the sensitivity of future developments to chance historic events – is central to understanding the failures of economic forecasting. See p 167.

# It's cool to be rich

4 SEPTEMBER 2003

As the hottest European summer most people can remember comes to an end, it is a timely moment to consider why cool countries are rich and hot countries poor. The most productive economies of the world are all located in temperate zones. The three exceptions serve to prove the rule. Hong Kong and Singapore are city states that became prosperous only after the advent of air conditioning. And the tropical area of Australia includes much of its landmass but very little of its population.

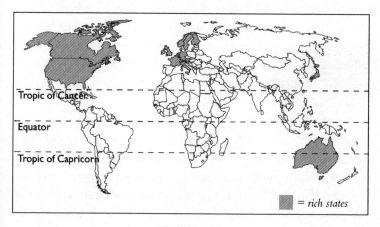

*Cool but rich*

The simplest explanation is that we are less disposed to work when it is hot. But when the quarterly GDP figures for sweltering Europe are published in the autumn, they will not be down by much. This is partly a problem of measurement. If a teacher is in front of a class, we assume everyone is doing something, though they may only be  sweating and waiting for the bell to ring. But we do measure the phone calls answered, the cars assembled, and the parcels delivered, as well as the ice cream eaten and the beer drunk. The overall impact of the heatwave on output will be very small relative to established  differences in national income between rich and poor.

Jeffrey Sachs, one of the few economists to have investigated the relationship between climate and growth, attributes much to the effect of disease. Sub-Saharan Africa has long been ravaged by malaria, and is today ravaged by AIDS, and these illnesses do great economic damage. But we need to think carefully about causation. Diseases which caused similar havoc in Britain, such as smallpox and plague, have been eliminated: much of the US was once malarial.

Rich countries have remedied most medical conditions that stop people working before old age. And they have been able to do so because they are rich. It is morally uncomfortable, even despicable, that we devote so much more resource to the minor ailments of affluence – depression and stomach ulcers – than to the life-threatening diseases of poverty – malaria and bilharzia. But we do.

Another explanation – differences in agricultural techniques – confronts the same problem of causality. Farming is more productive in rich countries, and the seeds and animals we use today are well adapted to temperate latitudes. But modern agriculture was invented in Iraq. Historians write about the fertile crescent of Mesopotamia as though it were a different place, and in a relevant sense it was. The United States is able to invade Iraq, but Iraq unable to invade the United States: not because of differences in endowments or technology, but because of differences in the effectiveness with which these endowments and technology have been used.

And it is to how resources are employed that we must look for explanation. Rich countries are not rich because they are specially blessed by their natural environments. If you were leading a mission to find the economic promised land you would probably not stop in Finland, Switzerland or Minnesota. But all of these areas have become affluent. It is not terrain that matters but people, culture, and institutions.

The modern market economy is a west European invention, and is most fully developed in Western Europe itself and in the areas which West Europeans settled. The ideal climate for emigrants is one a little better than, but not very different from, the one to which they are accustomed. That is why European settlers went to the North American seaboards, the south east coast of Australia, the north island of New Zealand, and the cape of South Africa. These same instincts explain why Germans went to Minnesota but the British did not. And all these emigrants brought the values and the social, political and economic institutions of the countries from which they came.

When Europeans arrived in the Congo, or Indonesia, they had come to loot, not to settle, because they found the weather uncomfortable and the environment threatening. Their guns were just as effective as at home but their seeds were not. They had neither aspiration nor capacity to reproduce the economic and political structures with which they were familiar, and they returned home without having done so. These areas remain poor today.

Yet there is one – only one – country which has developed a prosperous modern economy without importing European settlers and European institutions. Is it a coincidence that Japan is also located in a temperate zone? Probably – but I wish I could be sure.

------

The countries marked on the map are the richest countries in the world as identified in *The Truth about Markets* (chapter 3) and *Culture and Prosperity* (chapter 4). Jeffrey Sachs' discussion can be found in 'Institutions don't rule: direct effects of geography on *per capita* income', National Bureau of Economic Research Working Paper 9490, January 2003.

# The economics of immigration

21 MAY 2002

The views people hold on the economic effects of immigration seem to be entirely conditioned by their other social and political opinions. The left stresses the benefits, the right the costs. I have been looking for facts.

Is it better to be densely or sparsely populated? Rich Holland and poor Bangladesh are the most crowded countries in the world. Zaire and Australia cope very differently with rich mineral resources and low population densities. Is it better to have a rising population or a falling one? Across the twentieth century, population rose in Japan, fell in Germany, and remained much the same in France. Good economic institutions cope with most external circumstances. Bad ones fail, however favourable the circumstances.

Population growth probably led to the invention of agriculture ten thousand years ago, and made available the labour for Britain's industrial revolution. But it may be best to have the resources and infrastructure of a large population shared by a few. The peasants who survived the Black Death did relatively well out of it: and imagine how pleasant London would be if only half as many people lived there.

But these conditions do not last long. Population grew again after the Black Death. A modern-day London with lower house prices and uncrowded journeys to work would attract new residents. Economic systems are self-adjusting.

The economic effects of immigration depend, not on population growth or density, but on the characteristics of the immigrants themselves. While every mouth brings a pair of hands, these hands sometimes make more than they eat and sometimes less. Most migrants are of working age. People of working age have children and grow old, so this is not an indefinite benefit, but immigration always yields potential short term benefits if immigrants are immediately assimilated. Like the young Australians, Irish and New Zealanders who seem to occupy all the temporary secretarial and accounting jobs in London. With no problems of language or cultural adaptation, they are immediately more productive than the average Briton.

But most immigrants are not so easily absorbed. They generally earn less than indigenous workers of similar age and education: this difference diminishes over time but does not necessarily disappear, and may continue into a second generation. This may partly reflect racial discrimination, but also hard economics: people are less productive in an unfamiliar environment. Immigrants typically earn more than in their country of origin − that is why they migrate − but less than a native of the receiving country would earn with the same skills. This is the central economic fact about immigration. From it most social consequences as well as economic consequences follow.

There is not much migration between rich countries: but since there are billions of people who would be better off in the US or Western Europe than in their home countries, the problem is less to explain why there is so much attempted migration than why there is so little. But happiness depends less on absolute living standards than on the quality of life relative to expectations. That is why so many migrants come from failed states − such as Afghanistan or Eastern Europe − or from minorities who, like Huguenots, Jews and East African Asians, are often persecuted because they are economically successful. The distinction between economic migrants and political refugees is fine indeed.

If immigrants are generally paid less than the natives, what effect does this have on the earnings of the natives themselves? Studies of neighbourhoods that received substantial immigration − Cubans in  Miami and Algerians in Provence − show that local

wages did not fall. But this is not quite sufficient: if local wages had fallen, both immigrants and natives would have gone elsewhere. The critics' allegation is less that immigrants bid down wages, but that they take jobs. And that claim is hard to argue with. What we do not know definitively is whether jobs for other groups are eliminated or just displaced.

On balance, immigration usually produces economic benefits for the receiving country. Immigrants are more economically active than the native population: are paid less than natives with similar skills: are more energetic than natives, and more willing to take undesirable jobs, such as those with unsocial hours.

But these advantages are won at a high price. Relatively liberal immigration policies, which allow substantial unskilled immigration, create an underclass of people who are paid less than native workers, have grounds for feeling discriminated against, and may well in fact be discriminated against. From this resentment, familiar political and social problems grow.

Relatively strict immigration policies ensure that we import only highly skilled people. When they have been ejected, or come from countries whose political and economic chaos means their skills cannot be used effectively, this must be as good for the importing country as it is good for them. But when we recruit doctors, nurses and computer programmers from countries which are recipients of our foreign aid, we need to ask whether this is really a responsible policy for us to adopt.

It always comes back to politics.

---

A short reading list on the economics of immigration:

George J. Borjas, (1994), *The economic benefits from immigration*, National Bureau of Economic Research, Cambridge, Mass.

George J. Borjas (ed.), (2000), *Issues in the economics of immigration*, University of Chicago Press, Chicago.

Jonathan Coppel, Jean-Christophe Dumon and Ignazio Visco, (2001), *Trends in immigration and economic consequences*, OECD, Paris.

Ricardo Faini, Jaime de Melo and Klaus Zimmermann (eds.), (1999) , *Migration, the controversies and the evidence*, Centre for Economic Policy Research, Cambridge.

Timothy J. Hatton, Jeffrey G. Williamson, (1998), *The age of mass migration: causes and economic impact,* Oxford University Press, New York, Oxford

Mancur Olson, (1996), 'Big bills left on the sidewalk: why some nations are rich, and others poor,' *Journal of Economic Perspectives*, Spring, pp. 3-21.

Jeffrey G. Reitz, (1998), *Warmth of the welcome, the social causes of economic success for immigrants in different nations and cities*, Westview Press, Boulder, Colorado.

Julian L. Simon,(1989), *The economic consequences of immigration*, Basil Blackwell in association with the Cato Institute, Oxford.

# Geography still matters

10 JANUARY 2001

It is almost a cliché that geography is no longer relevant to economics. And evidence of globalisation is all around us. McDonalds is ubiquitous; multinational companies ruthlessly source their products from the cheapest locations. The internet has established a single worldwide community of information.

And yet the largest influence on the lifestyle you can expect is still your place of birth. Those born in Western Europe enjoy the highest material national standard of living achieved in human history. Children in sub-Saharan Africa or the Indian sub-continent can expect a much shorter lifespan, in grinding poverty little different from the experience of their distant ancestors.

Where you live is almost as important as where you are born. Immigrants to poor countries mostly enjoy living standards as high as they would in their country of origin. Otherwise they would not go. The standards of living of immigrants in rich economies are a blend of those of their birthplace and their adopted country. Germans in the United States have German or American incomes: Haitians in America earn more than they would in Haiti but less than the average American. Of course, the Germans are running DaimlerChrysler while the Haitians are more often kitchen porters.

The location of production still matters, but it matters in a different way. Once, most of what we consumed was produced near to where we live. Now, it is produced where there is competitive advantage, and the location of competitive advantage is often geographical. It is not just that sugar comes from Barbados and oil from Saudi Arabia: cameras mostly come from Japan, ties from Italy, and software from the United States.

And the most striking feature of electronic communication is not how much geographical diffusion of activities it has produced, but how little. Market trading, now screen-based, does not require that traders gather in a single location. But clusters of screens are sited within a few hundred yards of each other in densely packed and expensive areas of the City of London and lower Manhattan. And most received wisdom is that the financial services industry will become still more concentrated in a small number of centres. The attempt to consolidate European bourses is the product of the belief that regional market centres will not survive. Technology permits dispersion: but that dispersion is not happening.

Geography matters because even if the distribution of natural resources is no longer of overriding importance, the distribution of man-made resources is. The distribution of capital influences both standards of living and the location of business. Not just capital in the narrow sense of investment in plant and machinery, but human capital – investment in education – and social capital – the political and legal infrastructure and culture of personal relationships within which business is done. And the distribution of such capital today is as uneven as the distribution of natural resources was at the beginning of the industrial revolution.

Yet the distribution of capital, particularly physical capital, is not set by nature, but determined by people. With freedom of capital movement, its owners can locate capital where they will and they do not do so on nationalistic or patriotic grounds. Which is why differences in social capital are crucial. In a globalised world of freely moving capital and increasingly freely moving people, only social capital remains tied to specific locations.

These differences in institutions are the main influence on differences in living standards. And differences in social institutions also explain the localisation of what would otherwise seem to be footloose production. Tacit skills and knowledge are developed where people exchange ideas with each other casually and daily. Flexible production relationships are based on personal relationships.

The information that can be handled by information technology is of a limited kind. Some of the data needed in financial services can be found on screens. But much cannot. Such communication needs not only body language, but nuances that can be conveyed only between people who are, or have been, in the same room. The chat room is impoverished human interaction, and e-mail impoverished human communication.

So geography continues to be influential because of the continuing influence of history. Tie manufacture is centred in Italy, software production in the United States, and financial services are strong in England because capabilities that can be traced back to the social and economic histories of the respective countries – the flourishing of design skills in Italy during the Renaissance, the early development of a large installed base of computers in the United States, the pivotal role of English merchants in the development of trading economies.

It is more fortuitous that these activities are more specifically located near Lake Como, in Silicon Valley, and between Holborn and Aldgate. But such accidents of history are not easily reversed. As the evolution of London investment banking in the last decade has shown, the identity of the participants may change, but the location of the activity does not. So long as culture matters, history and geography will matter too.

# Risks and decisions

In 1947, Paul Samuelson published *Foundations of Economic Analysis* (definitely not to be confused with his introductory textbook, *Economics*). Samuelson's analysis provided a clear statement of the basic principles of neoclassical economics. With the general equilibrium framework of Kenneth Arrow and Gerard Debreu, this offered a consistent and coherent body of doctrine based on rational choice, and dominated the thinking of professional economists for the remainder of the century.

But more and more reasons for doubting the postulate of rationality have come to light. It is hard to have lived through the era of the 'new economy' and still believe that well informed, considered choices are normal in making economic decisions. Players in the stock market bubble were poorly informed about the past, and even more poorly informed about the future. The economics of information, and behavioural economics, are concerned with how people really make personal and business choices under uncertainties. Several of the essays here are particularly concerned with the complexities and apparent irrationalities of our behaviour towards risk.

# How we decide

15 MAY 2003

The Treasury's assessment of the consequences of British adoption of the euro is one of the most extensive cost benefit analyses ever undertaken. There will be numerous equations, copious data, and thousands of pages. The credentials of its authors suggest that the assessment will be carefully planned, technically skilled, and as fairly presented as is possible on such a politically controversial subject – the epitome of what modern civil servants are proud to call evidence-based policy.

And yet we know that it is all a charade. I have not met a single person who is genuinely waiting to read the assessment before deciding. Not one. I count some odd people among my friends. People who tremble with excitement before the release of the third quarter's manufacturing production figures. People whose idea of a good night out is an evening at the computer centre running econometric models.

But economists have been falling over themselves to take up positions in advance of the Chancellor's statement. And if that's true of economists, it is far more true of ordinary people. Go down to the pub and ask what customers think about the euro. You will get plenty of views, but I bet not one of them will be "I want to see what the Treasury has to say about Gordon Brown's third test".

Most people, in fact, will judge the assessment by newspaper reports. And we already know what these reports will say. Proprietors, editors and journalists have already made up their minds, and so have politicians. People will use the material in the assessment to reinforce the views they already hold, not to form their opinions, or to change them. And I doubt if discussion about the euro between Prime Minister Tony Blair and Chancellor Gordon Brown are much concerned with the statistical analysis contained in the assessment.

Big decisions in politics and business are the result of political horse-trading, and are based on partial information, visions and prejudices, hopes and fears.

We are taught that matters should be different. We would prefer to think that the right answer is deduced from dispassionate technical analysis. And so our leaders pretend that is what they are doing. They assure us the government's decision on euro membership will be based on an objective application of the Chancellor's five tests. Businesses tell us that they decide on big investments or strategic acquisitions only after they have calculated the discounted cash flow and undertaken extensive scenario modelling. But any competent civil servant or business analyst knows that his job is to work out the answer the boss wants and adjust assumptions accordingly.

It can never be otherwise. A British decision to join a single currency will last forever. And even with fifty years of hindsight, we will not know the answer. How could we ever tell what would have happened in an alternative scenario? The eurozone economies have performed poorly since the euro was launched. But perhaps they would have done worse if it had not been formed. The only thing we know for sure is that the assertions of those who anticipated either triumph or disaster were wrong.

Some people are instinctively internationalist, others regard national identity as a vital aspect of their lives. Some people are natural Europeans, others feel more at home with the language and values of the United States. There is nothing shameful about emotions of liking and disliking, nothing inappropriate about basing judgements on instincts about who can be trusted. Business people as well as politicians use the language of economics to make firm assertions about matters of which they can have very little knowledge.

We should resist pressures that require us to cloak these judgements in the language of economic costs and benefits. Such analyses may be helpful in framing our thoughts and revealing inconsistencies in our arguments, but they should not be the basis of our decisions. And in reality, they never are.

---

When Gordon Brown became Chancellor of the Exchequer in 1997, he laid down five economic tests which would have to be satisfied before the government would recommend Britain's entry into the euro. On 9 June 2003 the Treasury published a detailed assessment in 18 volumes and 2000 pages, which concluded that the tests had not yet been satisfied but that the issues would remain under review.

# An economist's tale:
# The deadweight loss of Christmas

13 DECEMBER 2000

You will not be receiving Christmas presents from me this year. Instead I am sending you a copy of the American Economic Review for 1993. It contains a fine article by Professor Joel Waldfogel entitled *The Deadweight Loss of Christmas*.

Professor Waldfogel's argument is simple. Suppose I give you a tie that cost me $50. It is unlikely that you would have bought exactly that tie if I had given you a $50 note. The difference in value between what I bought and what you would have done with the money is a measure of the inefficiency of gift giving – the deadweight loss of Christmas.

The American Economic Review encourages its contributors to support their analysis with data. Professor Waldfogel meets this requirement. A survey of 86 gift recipients found that they would have been willing to pay an average of $313 for the Christmas gifts they received. But the ungrateful interviewees estimated the total cost of these gifts to the donors at $438. Another sample would have been willing to sell their Christmas presents for an average of $462. This group estimated the average expenditure by donors at $509. Presents from aunts, uncles and grandparents were particularly inefficient. On average they were worth less than two-thirds of their cost. Gifts from friends and close family members did somewhat better.

Applying these results to the overall incidence of gift-giving in the United States, Professor Waldfogel estimated that the total loss to the American economy attributable to Christmas in 1992 alone was between \$4 billion and \$13 billion. Nor is that all. In the interest of political correctness, Professor Waldfogel reminds us that references to the deadweight loss of Christmas should be understood to apply equally to Hanukkah and other holidays with gift-giving rituals.

Professor Waldfogel's opus is in a tradition of pursuing the concept of rational economic man to dotty extremes. There are two ways of reacting to it. One is to take the view that there are certain areas of life which are off limits to economists. The assumption that people act as selfish maximisers may be helpful in explaining how business works but there are very large areas of social activity – such as Christmas – that need to be analysed in different ways. There is not – and there cannot be – any economics of beauty, goodness and truth.

But there is something unsatisfactory about a framework of analysis that imposes a dichotomy between the values of the business world and those of everyday life. It is humanly very difficult to be a beast in the board room and a saint at home. The expectation that one set of attitudes will inevitably corrode the other is the basis of much popular distaste for business, and provides a powerful rationale for an insistence that business values be kept away from nurturing activities such as education and healthcare. Christmas at the Waldfogels would be an impoverished affair.

Better to look for explanations of human behaviour that are comprehensive. Gifts are part of business life as well as social life. We give because it is conventional, and because it gives us pleasure both to give and to receive. But why is it conventional to exchange gifts, and why do we take pleasure in it? A gift is a demonstration of our commitment to a relationship. That is why it is unusual, but not unknown, for us to make gifts to strangers. Generous people may wish to make their commitment to the society in which they live. But most feel the strongest commitment to individual members with whom they are acquainted. The pleasure we take in the exchange of gifts is in the affirmation or

*Just what they always wanted*

reaffirmation of these commitments. Such pleasure is usually enough to override Professor Waldfogel's inefficiency – the knowledge that we will never actually want to wear the tie we unwrap on Christmas morning.

The connection between the gift and the relationship means that the gift should be appropriate. Too small a gift demeans the value we place on the relationship. Too large a gift appears to impose an obligation greater than the other party wishes to accept. The best gifts are those that reflect some intimate knowledge and demonstrate the special nature of the relationship. That may be the reason that Professor Waldfogel found that friends gave more efficient gifts than uncles and aunts.

There are still a few shopping days left before Christmas. Perhaps I will put down my copy of the American Economic Review and go to Harrods after all.

---

Professor Waldfogel's analysis can be found in 'The deadweight loss of Christmas', *American Economic Review*, Vol. 83, No. 5 December, 1993.

# Rational economic man

15 MARCH 2000

Economists still analyse the behaviour of rational economic man. He is constantly maximising. At work, he steers a balance between the pain of additional effort and the joy of additional reward. In the supermarket, he rushes from aisle to aisle comparing price and marginal utility. In the extreme variant put forward by some University of Chicago economists, this behaviour is universal. We refrain from stealing only when the expected penalty exceeds the value of the loot. We marry to gain economies of scale from living together. We commit suicide when the net value of future utility is no longer positive.

Students, and other critics, have always protested that no-one is really like that. Real people have family, friends and colleagues, and they care about them. Even when our economic behaviour is selfish, as it often is, it is as much concerned with our status and the respect of our peers as with material rewards.

Their teachers have offered two answers. One is that rational economic man is not necessarily self-centred, only consistent. When he gives money to beggars he is still maximising his utility: he shows only that the welfare of beggars is as much part of his utility as his own satisfactions. The weakness of this position is that it explains everything we have done after we have done it, but predicts nothing.

Another response is that the behaviour of rational economic man is an 'as if' hypothesis. We do not really have the single-minded objectives that the model assumes, but we mostly act as if we do. The reasoning is that the modern market economy favours rational economic man and rewards the decisions that rational economic man would make. So even if we are not naturally inclined that way, the behaviour of rational economic men becomes dominant.

Today's evolutionary biology shows how powerful such arguments can be. Our genes are not really selfish – they have no motives or intentions at all – but the hypothesis that they behave selfishly is a powerful way of understanding the process of evolution. What we call selfishness is simply the survival-oriented behaviour which is favoured by our environment. Yet there are two big differences between an evolutionary explanation of economic behaviour and the hypothesis of intrinsic rational self-centredness. One is that in evolutionary theory it is the gene, rather than the individual, that appears selfish. The other is that our evolutionary habits were acquired, not on Wall Street and at the Harvard Business School, but on the savannahs where modern economic man emerged from the apes.

Often, these differences are not significant. Idle man, who was discouraged by the labour of hunting and discounted the pleasures of the kill, did not prosper on the African grasslands. His genes were not spread widely. Nor were those of workaholic man, who expended more energy pursuing animals than he gained from eating his quarry, and returned home exhausted to find others had cornered all the women. Well-adjusted man, who judiciously balanced effort and reward, propagated his genes more effectively than either. And family man, who caught enough food to look after not only himself but his wife and children, did best of all. That kind of rational economic man also does well in modern society.

But other things have changed. There was little need or opportunity to assess probabilities on the savannah. When big game was in prospect, bands of tribesmen would hunt together. Perhaps that is why even today psychologists have found that we give disproportionate weight to the possibility of extreme but unlikely outcomes, and are unduly swayed by the enthusiasms of

others. These traits may have served us well in Africa 100,000 years ago, but can lead us astray when we buy a lottery ticket or subscribe for shares in lastminute.com.

Grassland hunting was more productive when groups of hunters pooled their knowledge of animal spoors and shared their catch. But here they faced the same dilemma that confronts rational economic man today. Co-operative behaviour was in the general, but not the individual, interest. Rational economic man took all the information he could from others but kept his own information for his own benefit.

Imagine two tribes, one of which is mainly made up of co-operative men. The other is populated by rational economic men. Co-operative man is friendly, with natural instincts to socialise at work and to share his good fortune with others. Rational economic man is always calculating his own advantage. Rational economic men hunt alone, because although they understand the benefits of working together, they always cheat on each other. Co-operative tribes catch more animals per head. And the more food they gather, the more people like them there will be in subsequent generations.

If – as must also have been true in our ancestors' time – tribes consisted of mixtures of co-operative men and rational economic men, then the analysis is more complex. The best situation of all is to be the only rational economic man in a tribe of co-operative men. But that is only if your genial colleagues cannot identify your true nature. When they do, you will find yourself on your own. Tribes will divide into co-operative and non-co-operative groups, and the former will usually eat better.

So genetics favours co-operative man over rational economic man. Man is a social animal. This is not simply a cliché, but an observation by biologists who have compared human behaviour with that of other species. And if man were not a social animal he would not be as economically successful as he has been. People who marry because they have genuine love and affection for others are more likely to pass on their genes than those who want to marry to reap economies of scale in household production. Rational economic man dies out because no-one much wants to mate with him.

---

Lastminute.com, the appropriately named archetype of European internet stocks, was floated at the peak of the stock market in 2000 at a price of 380p per share. The offer was heavily oversubscribed and individual applicants were rationed to 35 shares each. The shares subsequently fell to 18p: but, using the cash raised from punters to buy established travel agencies, the company subsequently transformed itself into a modest sustainable business.

Accounts of the evolutionary models described here can be found in Robert Frank (1988), *Passions within Reason*, Alton.

# The Taleb distribution

16 JANUARY 2003

I've been driving in France again. I've been tailgated, overtaken on the inside. More than once I only just avoided a driver on the wrong side of a blind mountain bend. Why do they do it? I used to think that French drivers could behave like that because they knew their roads better than I did. The broken glass, the dented cars, tell another story. And so do the statistics. Despite the empty roads of rural France, there are so many more accidents that the French transport minister has recently taken the extreme step of imploring his compatriots to drive 'commes les anglais'.

The practice of bad driving has what I call a Taleb distribution, after one of the themes in Nassim Nicholas Taleb's brilliant *Fooled by Randomness*. A Taleb distribution has the property that many small profits are mixed with occasional large losses. Overtaking on the inside is an activity with a Taleb distribution.

We engage in Taleb distributions because it is so easy to dissociate the losses from the profits. The losses are out of the normal run of things. The cars on the French tow trucks and the drivers in the back of the ambulances were victims of unforeseeable events. They suffered from what commercially minded accountants long ago christened exceptional items. The rule is that you don't match exceptional items against ordinary profits.

Taleb distributions are fine when you have experienced only the upside. A Taleb distribution led to the crises in the Lloyds insurance market. Excess of loss policies – the LMX spiral – insured other syndicates against losses of unprecedented magnitude. The underwriters pointed out that they had taken in premiums for many years and paid nothing out. You do not have to be as smart as Taleb to see the flaw, but you do have to be a little smarter than the Feltrim and Gooda Walker syndicates. There are other, less abstruse examples. Drinking more than is good for us has a Taleb distribution. So does smoking – after all, most smokers don't get lung cancer.

Many apparently successful traders and business people are still on the upside of their Taleb distribution. They are accidents waiting to happen. It puzzled me for years that so many organisations believed they were making money out of proprietary trading in securities markets. These businesses were dealing mostly with each other: since there is no perpetual motion, where did the money to fuel the system come from? From Taleb distributions.

Arbitrage in financial markets generates a continuing stream of small profits. Large losses are exceptional items. They are the product of misjudgements, rogue traders, unpredictable events, and the failures of risk control. The same misjudgements, rogue drivers, unpredictable events and system failures that lead to crashes on the French autoroutes.

We find Taleb distributions not only on the road and in financial institutions. Hedge funds make them accessible to a general public. Business people learned centuries ago that you can water the milk again, and again, and again. Until Taleb strikes back: people notice and take their custom elsewhere. Marks and Spencer, the retailer, pushed to the limit of what its customers could stand until they discovered they had crossed that limit. Banks have treated their account holders the same way. Eventually, you pass on the inside once too often.

Evolution allows Taleb distributions to persist. The gene pool of dreadful French drivers is depleted by road accidents, but only at the rate of 8000 a year. Most young Frenchmen make it to their dates. And evolution within organisations has a similar bias. Someone who makes steady small gains ranks as a safe pair of hands, and is promoted till he meets his apotheosis.

Can we escape the Taleb problem? Understanding risk is the

prelude to managing it. We know instinctively that the tailgating driver is not really smart, and nor is the high yield bond trader. Taleb himself exploits his distribution by looking for its opposite: trading strategies in securities markets that offer frequent small losses and occasional large gains. His insight is that no financial institution will tolerate people who lose money nine days out of ten. Just as French drivers will not tolerate the safe motorist who slows them down. I hope that Mrs Taleb will continue to be indulgent.

------

Nicholas Nasim Taleb's *Fooled by Randomness* was published by Texere in 2002.

# Not in our stars

11 NOVEMBER 1998

'The fault, dear Brutus, is not in our stars, but in ourselves, that we are underlings.' Cassius was not on his way to buy insurance when he said this. But if he had been, he would have understood why he could insure against being struck by lightning, but not against banishment. And those who read his words today will appreciate why they are regularly offered financial protection against damage to property or personal injury, but not divorce, pregnancy or redundancy. The answer lies in the difference between the faults in ourselves and the faults in our stars.

A bolt of lightning is truly a random event, and an insurance company which pools a lot of these risks can be fairly confident of the outcome. But divorce, pregnancy and redundancy are events which are partly under individual control, and the people who may experience these events know better how likely they are than any insurance company. If you want to insure against becoming pregnant, I don't want to sell you the policy.

What are the relative roles of personal responsibility and unpredictable misfortune? How much do we know about ourselves relative to what others know, and how reliably can they find it out? When Caesar had been warned to beware the Ides of March, did that change the allocation of blame for his fate between himself and the conspirators? The answers to these questions differentiate those risks that can and should be left to the private insurance market – like fire and theft – from those – abrupt loss of office – that typically fall on individuals themselves. In many countries these latter risks are partly picked up by the state, which offers benefits to lone parents, mothers and their

*So, honey, you forgot to renew the divorce insurance*

children, and those who lose their jobs. So we define the border-lines between private and social insurance.

Where risks are not random, we generally need to worry about fault. If, as in the United States, there is very little social insurance to cover personal risks, then the only way you can avoid bearing them yourself is to attribute blame to someone else. That is an important reason why America is such a litigious society.

In European countries, where social insurance is more extensive, we try to limit provision, though not to eliminate it, for those whose plight is their own fault. So we withhold some benefit from people who left jobs voluntarily, we are unsympathetic to divorcees without children, and we agonise over how supportive we should be of lone parents. In all these cases, our society's assessment of the relative contribution of individual responsibility and genuine misfortune governs the generosity of our social insurance provision.

And it is why in most countries outside the United States, medical insurance has in effect been nationalised. Ill-health has some of the characteristics of fire, and some of the characteristics of divorce. There are elements of luck in the incidence of any illness. But there are also elements of personal responsibility. And even if there is no fault, nor is there randomness. It is not very difficult to assess that some people are more likely to fall ill than others, by virtue of their age, their lifestyle, or the knowledge that they themselves have.

In sectors such as these, private insurance markets tend to unravel, as insurers adopt direct and indirect ways of picking off the better risks. Many people are left uninsured, and the system does best when employers insure on behalf of large, undifferentiated groups of customers. Private medical insurance only works well either when it is based around employers or where, as in most countries, its operation is so regulated by government that it really constitutes a health service rather than a private insurance market.

The nature of the risks that individuals face, the difference between true misfortune and personal responsibility, and what we know about the risks we face relative to what others know, are fundamental to the design of our social, economic and political institutions. They are the most important factors determining the boundaries between the public and private sector, the design of the social security system, and the degree of state involvement in many important activities such as health and employment.

That is why this week's announcement that the British government wants to work with the insurance industry on a voluntary code to evaluate genetic testing is much more significant than it seems. We see the opening of a Pandora's box, and you cannot peek inside and shut it again. No attempts to reverse the march of technology, or to suppress knowledge we already have, have succeeded for long.

As our knowledge of genes grows, we change the boundaries between what we think is determined for us and what is a matter of our own choice and responsibility. And we alter the distinction between what we know about ourselves and what others can know about us. Most immediately, this will be relevant to life and medical insurance, as what have hitherto been random, and hence insurable, events become systematically more predictable. This is simply an inevitable part of most advances in medical technology, and it is why insurance markets are not ultimately a viable solution to the problems of ill-health, pensions or long-term care.

But the full ramifications go wider. It is no more true that I commit crimes because of my criminal genes than it is true that my crimes are all the fault of society. But there is enough in both contentions to make it ultimately impossible to distinguish clearly nature, nurture and personal responsibility. Yet it is not just our social attitudes, but our economic institutions – from the welfare state to the commercial legal system – that depend on that distinction. The more we learn about either sociology or genetics, the more tenuous the distinction becomes.

# Stocks for the long run

9 DECEMBER 1998

It has been a good century for equity investors. Barclays Capital are proud keepers of records of returns on different asset classes since 1918. Over that period, British equities have outperformed cash and bonds by around 6% per annum. This finding is very robust. Over all but the shortest time periods this outperformance – the equity premium – has been consistently maintained. Research in the US suggests a similar figure has been true there.

The economic consequences have been profound. Institutional investment, once dominated by fixed interest holdings, is today mainly in shares. Financial markets and corporate governance are organised around the central role of equity markets. Companies seek returns on investment that match equity investors' expectations – 15% or more. So they look for deals, and narrow the range of their activities to focus on those that will assure these high returns. We invest relatively much less in infrastructure than our Victorian forebears.

There are good reasons why equities should yield more than safe assets. Risk is the essence of capitalism. The equity premium is what shareholders need to be paid for lying awake at night, tossing and turning, worrying about the fate of their investments. They could place their money on deposit, or in indexed bonds, and sleep more soundly. Bravely, they have chosen not to. They need to be compensated for this disturbance to their tranquillity.

But at 6% per year? The UK stock market is capitalised at £1250 billion. That makes the annual compensation for loss of sleep £75 billion. About 10% of national income and £1300 per year for each man, woman and child in the country. And since most of these men, women and children do not give a moment's thought to the level of the stock market, the rest of us must be losing a lot of well-remunerated sleep.

Indeed, the rewards of risk-bearing are so high as almost to eliminate the risk itself. If equities outperform safe assets by 6% a year then the probability that you will do better in safe assets than in equities over a ten year period is negligible. This is the equity premium puzzle. The equity premium is the reward for risk, but the magnitude of the reward is wholly out of line with the magnitude of the risk.

However you look at it, the equity premium is inexplicably high. What would happen if such returns persisted? The net yield on the All-Share index, which is what investors will receive next century, is today about 0.5% more than the secure return on indexed gilts. To provide a total return 6% higher than a safe investment in indexed stock, company earnings and dividends will have to grow at 5.5% per year – indefinitely. But the British economy does not grow at anything like this rate, and nor can profits and share prices. If they did, by the end of next century dividends would absorb more than half of national income and compensation for worrying about the level of share prices would be the main source of national income.

We can say, with certainty, that equity returns will not be as high in future as in the past and that people who look for 15% returns on assets are living a dream. That means that the last hundred years, in which the outperformance of equities has been a consistent theme, have been a fluke, an aberration. Hard to believe. Still, the improbable is more likely than the impossible.

So has the impossible come to pass? A whole series of special factors has favoured equity investments. Some have been long-term trends. Inflation has been faster than anticipated across most of the century. Quoted companies have become a far more important part of the economy. Short-term influences have also boosted shares. The re-rating of equities relative to other investments, rapid growth in productivity, a recognition of the importance of knowledge-based assets.

Few of these factors favouring equities were fully apprehended before they happened. Imagine yourself seeking investment advice in 1900. Your uncle might have advised Buenos Aires tramways: Argentina then seemed the coming place. Your grandfather might have recommended Russian bonds: however unattractive the Tsar's regime, he offered a security unavailable in volatile democracies. Your cousin would have had confidence in farmland. And your father would have assured you of the stability of residential property. There would always be a need for central London mansions, and Shropshire estates. Perhaps a raffish great uncle might have recommended to you a small wager on the Atlanta pharmacist whose Coca-Cola beverage was catching on in the Southern states.

If you had taken him seriously, you would have more than compensated for the huge losses you would have incurred on the other, more prudent, suggestions. With the benefit of hindsight, we know that shares in British and American companies were the outstanding investments of the twentieth century. But that is with the benefit of hindsight: in 1900, other people were buying Argentinian tramways. And they might have been right in their investment decisions. If they had been, small investors would today be piling into tramway investments and we would be reading academic treatises on the tramway premium puzzle.

Past performance is not a guide to the future, as the advertisements say. We do not know what asset class will perform best over the next century because if we did, that knowledge would already be reflected in the price. Your best strategy in 1900 was to take some, but not too much, of the advice of all your relatives. Diversification remains the only key to security of investment performance.

Maybe this is the end of the century of equity outperformance. But do not rush to sell your holdings. It is almost fifteen years since two financial economists, Mehra and Prescott, first drew the attention of the academic world to the equity premium puzzle. They argued that it was much higher than rational economic theory could explain. The longest bull market in the history of investment followed.

---

The equity premium paradox was formulated by R. Mehra and E.C. Prescott, (1985),' The Equity Premium: a puzzle', *Journal of Monetary Economics*, 15, March, pp 145-61. An extensive survey of long run returns from stocks can be found in Dimson, E., Marsh, P., and Staunton, M.,(2002), *Triumph of the Optimists: 101 Years of Global Investment Returns*, Princeton University Press. There were further substantial rises in world stock markets in 1999 before peaks, not yet regained, were reached in early 2000.

# Chain letters

3 MAY 2000

From the earliest days of market economies, there have been financial promoters with a single objective. To persuade people to give them more money than they intend to give back.

The simplest route to lazy riches has always been to lie. I can create precious metals from base materials. There is undiscovered gold in the unexplored wilderness of Indonesia. Ostriches are a neglected source of delicious meat and nutritious protein. A few suckers are always attracted to these propositions, but the likelihood of exposure and imprisonment deters most people from advancing them.

The better trick is therefore to receive more than you pay out while being honest and open about what you are doing. This requires redistribution: some people get more than they put in, others less. Those who enter the scheme must believe they are likely to be in the category who will receive more, rather than in the category who will receive less. This cannot, in aggregate, be true. But the objective is to rely on self- deception by the participants, rather than overt deception by the promoters.

Virtually all schemes that have been devised fall into one of three categories – redistribution to the early, redistribution to the lucky, redistribution to the skilful. These correspond to chain letters, lotteries, and games. In each case, thoughtful players may understand that taken as a whole they will lose, but can still believe they will not be among the people who do.

Chain letters depend on an ever expanding circle of participants. Dodgy banks, from the first days of money lending to the Bank of Credit and Commerce International in our own times,

have always used this principle. You pay withdrawals and generous interest from the savings of new depositors.

These activities are illegal because they promise generous interest. The safer route is simply to create the expectation of high return from the evidence of the success of those who joined the scheme early. Financial chain letters are now generally known as Ponzi schemes (after Charles Ponzi, who developed a celebrated example in the US in the 1920s) or pyramid selling (after a group of companies who filled the garages of their victims with unwanted detergent in the 1970s).

As Robert Shiller notes in his recent guide to financial speculation, most Ponzi schemes offer some feeble explanation of how they generate their high return. Mr Ponzi claimed that large profits could be earned from international arbitrage in postal reply coupons. Pyramid sales people were assured that direct distribution was a means of undermining the excessive profits of soap powder manufacturers. Albanians, whose economy was brought to collapse by an explosion of Ponzi schemes, were told that the transition to capitalism would allow the widespread and effortless accumulation of riches. There are people who believe the same thing today about the internet.

Because Ponzi schemes inevitably end in collapse, governments are anxious to outlaw them. Their countermeasures usually rest on prosecuting the deception in the explanation. When a company called Titan Business Systems entered Britain with an entirely clean Ponzi scheme – they did not pretend that there was any source of revenue other than an ever-increasing number of new participants – it showed that no deception is needed to induce gullible people to take part. The very openness of the scam caused the Department of Trade and Industry difficulty in shutting it down.

Chain letters are possible because players can easily persuade themselves that they are early. It is almost as easy to persuade yourself that you are skilful. When people are asked to compare themselves to the norm – as drivers, lovers or executives of large corporations – less than half the population rates itself as below average. Some of the optimists are found in betting shops, studying form. Some of them are in casinos, believing – against reason and experience – that they can predict the movement of a roulette wheel.

Other optimists are in the trading-rooms of banks and large corporations. Foreign exchange trading, and secondary dealing in fixed interest securities, are – like roulette and racecourse betting – zero sum games, in which players can only win at the expense of losers. But in all these activities, a high proportion of partici-pants believe their own dealings are profitable. Mostly, their perception relies on systems – whether selective memory or accounting rules – that are more effective at recording gains than losses.

Lotteries are the most transparent and enduring means of

persuading people to part with more cash than you intend to return. It is harder to see how people can persuade themselves that they are more than averagely lucky than more than averagely early or skilful. But they manage it. They are also influenced by a psychological trait described as prospect theory. We focus on improbable outcomes to a degree that is not justified by their low probability. Economists call this irrational: but all they mean is that not many economists play lotteries and that running lotteries is a profitable business.

The most sophisticated financial schemes are those that combine elements of all three types. Day trading, for example. It is a game, at which I am skilful. It is a chain letter, in which I am an early participant. In time, other people will 'get it', and my holdings can be sold on at a higher price. And it is a lottery – we all agree that most new economy stocks will fail, but one or two will prove to be immensely valuable. There is one enduring and unvarying feature of all these schemes. It is better to run them than to participate.

---

Robert Shiller's book, *Irrational Exuberance*, was published by Princeton University Press at the peak of the stock market bubble in April 2000.

# Economic systems

Most people think that economics is about forecasting what will happen in foreign exchange markets, what will be in the budget, and what the central bank will do to interest rates. This section of the book is about the relationship between economics and politics, but it starts from the premise that questions such as these, even though they capture the attention of people in financial markets are neither the interesting nor the significant issues of political economy.

The idea that runs through this section is that what really matters to economic performance is the balance between centralisation and pluralism, between solidarity and individualism. Two groups of comparison figure particularly strongly – those between centrally planned and market economies, and those between Western Europe and the United States. The overriding theme is that the way in which an economy functions is the consequence, not just of technology and productive inputs, but of the society and culture in which economic institutions are embedded.

# Over the wall

3 JANUARY 1997

The claim of social sciences to be sciences is undermined by the difficulty of conduct controlled experiments. Physicists can create vacuums, chemists can establish sterile environments, even doctors can conduct blind trials. But economists, sociologists, political scientists and those who study management find their subject matter will never stand still.

But there has been one great controlled experiment in economics. Fifty years ago, one of the world's most successful economies was divided into two zones. In one, there was a powerful central planning agency, able to assess needs and co-ordinate production plans. In the other, people were left to do pretty much what they liked.

The experiment was conducted in Germany, and a few years ago the results came in. One third of the way through, it was necessary to build a wall to keep the experiment going, otherwise most of the inhabitants of one zone would have fled to the other. The end came when they tore down the wall and fled anyway. It is difficult to be exact, but most observers agree that by that time living standards in the West were at least twice those of the East.

One lesson is that the macroeconomic issues which typically preoccupy politicians and the press – what will happen to interest rates, how large is the budget deficit – are not really of much importance. West Germany had an exemplary record in the management of monetary and fiscal policy, but almost no one believes that this was why West Germany was rich and East Germany poor. The reasons were microeconomic, the different ways markets and industries were organised in the two zones.

History drives home the lesson that German macroeconomic

management was disciplined in the post-war period because German macroeconomic management had been undisciplined in the 1920s. For a time, there was no control at all over the currency or the level of public expenditure. The political consequences for Germany proved to be substantial, but the impact on German productive capacity was slight and temporary. No inflation has ever done the amount of damage to overall living standards achieved by East German planners.

So is the moral that politics should not be allowed to interfere with the process of production and exchange? There is something in that claim, but it also requires thoughtful interpretation. There were many things the East German regime had to worry about, but winning elections was not one of them. East Germany was quite unusually free from the clamour of tabloid headlines, from the exigencies of parliamentary debate, and from the electoral pressures which make the economic policies of western governments irresponsible and short-term in orientation.

In reality, East German production was controlled by a self-perpetuating bureaucracy. Neither in structure, nor in the background ability and training of those involved, was that organisation very different from the self-perpetuating bureaucracies that control large corporations in the West. Nor should we think that devotion to the cause of shareholder value was a more powerful spur to efficiency than the advancement of the dictatorship of the proletariat. Fortunately, neither rhetoric has much effect on what anyone actually does. Advancement in East Germany depended as much on obedience to prevailing orthodoxy as on evidence of performance on the job, but then isn't there something of that also in Siemens, Shell and General Electric?

The essential difference between East and West was that between centralisation and decentralisation of economic power. Much of the West German economy was also run by hierarchical political organisations, but there were many of them. Ideas neglected in one would be tried in another, and the easier comparison of performance made failures more obvious. The East, deprived of this process, made few drugs and lousy televisions. What went on a restaurant menu could be decided locally by people who knew their customers, not by a planning agency; the same reason explains why French hotels are better than Little Chefs. Fragmented structures facilitated innovation, processed more effectively the masses of information needed to run a modern economy, and made individuals responsible for the consequences of their own actions.

Yet this outcome is still surprising. It is and remains counter-intuitive that decentralised economic systems out-perform planned and co-ordinated ones. And it is only through experience that the efficiency of decentralisation has been recognised as an empirical as well as a theoretical truth. The Soviet Union was first into space: in the years that followed people on the right as well as the left feared that, morally repellent though the totalitarian regimes of Eastern Europe might be, they would be more successful economically.

We now know that this view is ludicrous, but have not fully taken the implications on board. We are still inclined to think that large firms, with co-ordinated massed resources, are bound to win out against diffuse and decentralised forms of organisation; that companies will benefit from a strong central authority with a well-defined common purpose. There is a striking resemblance between the cults of powerful chief executives, with their propagation of corporate visions, between the endless restruc-turing and change management programmes of modern corporations, and the political posturing of dotty dictators. No one should think that the superior performance of free enterprise economies over socialist ones came about because business people were wiser than politicians, or of superior moral stature. It's the economic system, stupid.

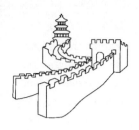

17 September 2003                                        Beijing

Dear Linda,

Yesterday was free for sightseeing. In Beijing's Forbidden City, one
courtyard leads on to another in a seemingly endless series. A brief
dash north took us to the Great Wall which winds along mountain
ridges for 2,500 miles. These wonders of the world are an illustration
of the tribute exacted from a poor population by an imperial court
concerned only with its own aggrandisement and preservation.

You climb to the Great Wall in a Swiss funicular, and we made the
hair-raising descent in a toboggan designed in Germany. In the
Mercedes limousine that took us back to Beijing, there was a chance
to debate one of the great paradoxes of economic history: China's
relative economic decline in the five centuries that followed the
construction of the Wall and the City monuments to the reign of the
Ming emperors.

The country that dynasty ruled was the technological equal of
Western Europe. Even at the end of the eighteenth century, the gap
between average incomes in China and in Europe was not large. In
technology and resources, south-east China and north-west Europe
were equally poised for economic development.

One of the embassy people had just finished reading The Great
Divergence, by Yale economic historian Ken Pomeranz. Europe, and
the fledgling United States, experienced the industrial revolution. But
nothing similar happened in China. The central element of
Pomeranz's explanation is that Europe had ample reserves of coal,
and China did not. But this is surely a proximate explanation rather
than a fundamental cause. Europeans had readier access to the

resources that were central to their particular course of economic development. China's resources were different: it exploited its great rivers as Europe had never done, or needed to. The fertile ingenuity of a developing economy makes use of whatever resources are to hand.

But the use of water involved central organisation, unlike the use of coal and steam. This points to a vital issue: Europe was a pluralist society in many ways that China was not. Today's visitor to China is daunted by the scale of a single country of 1.3 billion people, while Europe's 400 million are divided amongst dozens of states.

Unity is a benefit if you seek to marshal the scale of resources required to build the Great Wall. But that same unity works against diversity in intellectual life and political institutions, and variety of commercial and technological experiment. And the interaction of these processes of experiment and change is central to economic growth. Pluralism in ideas followed the European Renaissance, and spread to science and technology. Unified religious authority broke down with the Reformation. Centralised political power in Europe was only ever exercised in the short-lived successes of conquerors such as Napoleon.

> Now England is paying homage.
> They have out-travelled Shu-hai and Heng-chang;
> My Ancestors' merit and virtue must have reached
>     their distant shores.
> Though their tribute is commonplace,
> my heart approves sincerely.
> Curios and the boasted ingenuity of their devices
>     I prize not.
> Though what they bring is meagre, yet,
> In my kindness to men from afar I make generous
>     return,
> Wanting to preserve my prestige and power

*Poem composed by the Emperor Qianlong to commemorate the visit of a European mission to China in 1793.*

*In China, however, the Ming and Qing dynasties were successful for centuries in maintaining a single authority. And with that central control came the deliberate suppression of independent thought and local experiment. Imperial China gave the English language the term mandarin – an official whose fine intellectual skills, like those of Chinese bureaucrats, are directed not to the advancement of new ideas but to their critical scrutiny.*

*Emperor Qianlong exercised a degree of authority with few parallels in the history of the world – a centralism from which China has only recently begun to escape. When Chinese imperial power finally collapsed at the start of the twentieth century, it was replaced, not by disciplined pluralism, but by chaos. Mao's regime imposed still more dogmatic uniformity. Only when such uniformity broke down after his death did China begin to recognise the economic benefits of pluralism. And in the bustling streets around the Forbidden City today, you can see the formidable consequences.*

*John*

---

*The Great Divergence* by Ken Pomeranz was published in 2000 by Princeton University Press.

# Adam Smith and the invisible hand

24 SEPTEMBER 2003

There are few images of the founder of modern economics, Adam Smith. The best are the caricatures drawn by John Kay of Edinburgh, born in that city two centuries before I was. I was therefore particularly pleased when the National Portrait Gallery asked me to offer a pen portrait of the great man for its exhibition, 'Heroes and Villains'.

It led me to investigate the origins of his most famous phrase – 'the invisible hand'. The common modern interpretation of Smith's words is that 'the pursuit of self interest cumulatively adds up to the overall betterment of society'. This paraphrase is used in Daniel Yergin and Joseph Stanislaw's exultant account of the triumph of free markets *The Commanding Heights*.

Actually, the passage *The Wealth of Nations* which contains the metaphor is hardly a song of praise for liberal economics. Smith is arguing that import restrictions are unnecessary because British merchants will naturally prefer to buy from other British traders than entrust their fortunes to unreliable foreigners. Taken as a whole, it is neither the most profound nor the most elevating section of *The Wealth of Nations* and, but for that one observation, it would have been entirely forgotten.

The phrase 'the invisible hand' originates not with Smith, but with Shakespeare. Having ascended the Scottish throne through the killing of Duncan, Macbeth must cover his tracks by ordering the murder of Banquo. As dusk falls, the appointed time for the further crime approaches

> *'Come, seeling night,*
> *Scarf up the tender eye of pitiful day,*

*And, with thy bloody and invisible hand*
*Cancel and tear to pieces that great bond*
*Which keeps me pale'.*

Macbeth goes on to muse that 'Things bad begun make strong themselves by ill'. This sentiment would have been recognised in the boardrooms of Enron and WorldCom. And Shakespeare accurately anticipated the events that were to unfold in these businesses. Macbeth's hitmen succeed in killing Banquo, but Banquo's son escapes to England. The whistleblower exposes Macbeth's activities and returns to Scotland with an invading army which deposes the murderous king. The pursuit of self-interest not only fails to represent to the overall betterment of society: it ultimately destroys those who engage in it.

I don't know whether Macbeth was recently performed in Clintonville, Mississippi, or Houston, Texas. But Adam Smith knew the play well: he delivered public lectures on Shakespeare's imagery. Scholars such as Emma Rothschild and A.L. Macfie have argued that Smith was intrigued by the metaphor of the invisible hand, which recurs several times in his work.

The invisible hand ultimately steered Ken Lay and Bernie Ebbers to ends that were no part of their intention. Nor did their pursuit add up to represent the overall betterment of society. What would Adam Smith have thought of these individuals, and these events? Not much, we know. 'Commerce', he wrote, 'sinks the courage of mankind…. The minds of men are contracted, and rendered incapable of elevation'. Smith, it should be acknowledged, was a sceptical observer of all human behaviour. Politicians, doctors, and above all university professors, felt the lash of his acerbic tongue.

We can be sure that Smith did not intend to applaud today's Masters of the Universe. But we live in an economy inconceivably different from that of eighteenth century Scotland, and it is a mistake to foist parentage of modern ideas on him, or to seek insights into twenty-first century business from careful exegesis of his text.

*Adam Smith by John Kay*

But we can learn from Smith and other figures of the Scottish enlightenment a lesson common to all interpretations of the invisible hand. These eighteenth-century figures discerned a spontaneous order in economic and social systems, which would ultimately reassert itself even in the face of disruptive change. In the words of Smith's contemporary, Adam Ferguson, 'nations stumble on establishments which are the result of human action, but not of human design'.

The final curtain falls on a note of calm. The usurper is killed in action, Duncan's son, Malcolm, is proclaimed King of Scotland and promises

> *'this, and what needful else*
> *That calls upon us, by the grace of Grace,*
> *We will perform in measure, time and place'.*

The moral of Shakespeare's play, and of Smith's *magnum opus*, is not that selfish behaviour works for the public good. It is of the follies of human ambition, and of the failures of grand design. That moral is as relevant for our times as for Smith's, or Shakespeare's.

# Alexei Stakhanov meets Ken Lay

29 JUNE 2002

It is often said that socialism failed because it lacked incentives. But Soviet Russia had the greatest range of rewards and punishments imaginable – from the privileges of the *nomenklatura* to hard labour in the Gulag. Socialism failed because its incentives were perverse. If rewards and punishments are large enough people will try to meet the targets you set, but you will often wish they hadn't.

The story of the nail factory, which met its quota by producing one gigantic nail because that quota was based on weight of output, is probably apocryphal. But it identifies the general problem: whatever measure you choose, managers will focus on that measure at the expense of other equally important criteria. When Soviet production units or the economy as a whole fell seriously short of the plan, managers and their advisers responded by making the numbers up. It is a wry paradox that today's failures of capitalism so closely resemble yesterday's failures of socialism.

Incentivising managers to create value for shareholders has superficial attractions. But in the great stock market boom of the 1990s, companies had to report earnings growth in excess of 10% a year simply to maintain their share price. Even on the most optimistic analysis, the economy does not grow at 10% a year. How could companies operating in a competitive market have continually increased profits more rapidly than the growth of their underlying business? The simple answer is that while individual companies might, the business sector taken as a whole could not. The profits of established companies should grow more slowly than the world economy, because new businesses are constantly taking share from them. There is always scope for

*Heroes of the Soviet Union*

improving efficiency and introducing new technology, but in a competitive economy the benefits of greater efficiency and new technologies go to consumers. And the business environment is becoming more competitive, not less.

Analysts at investment banks struggled to square this circle: they explained how the genius of men like Ken Lay of Enron and Bernie Ebbers of WorldCom had changed the rules of the competitive game. Stalin's statisticians similarly recorded and applauded the heroic endeavours of individual Soviet workers such as Alexei Stakhanov, the apparently superhuman Siberian miner. They produced a rich tapestry of imaginary feats and bogus statistics, like the shareholder value movement fifty years later.

In the capitalist fantasy, companies achieved impossible earnings growth by cutting the fat from their businesses. Only gradually will it emerge how much bone and muscle they cut at the same time. The business of Marks and Spencer, the retailer, was unparalleled in reputation, but mature. To achieve earnings growth consistent with a glamour rating the company squeezed suppliers, gave less value for money, spent less on its stores. In 1998 it achieved the highest margin on sales in the history of the business. It had also compromised its position to the point where sales and profits plummeted.

Banks and insurance companies have taken staff out of branches and retrained those that remain as sales people. The pharmaceutical industry has taken advantage of mergers to consolidate its research and development facilities. Energy companies have cut back on exploration.

We know that these actions increased corporate earnings. We do not know what effect they had on the long run strength of the business, nor – and this is the key point – do the companies themselves know. Some rationalisations will genuinely lead to more productive businesses. Other companies will suffer the fate of Marks and Spencer. All we or they can say with confidence is that customer perceptions of retail financial service businesses are poor, that the pipeline of new drugs is smaller than it has been, that oil prospects look good mainly because of opportunities in the former Communist world.

Well established businesses, with strong competitive advantages, can use such tactics to take short-term profits at the expense of future growth. Newer companies without such opportunities have employed legitimate accounting wheezes. Acquisition accounting attributes little value to the assets you buy, so that you can flatter future profits by releasing the hidden value. And if you pay yourselves and your employees in stock options, you are allowed to leave the costs out of the profit and loss account.

But these devices require rising stock markets. Acquisition accounting is a drug; you need increasing doses to maintain your habit. After two years of falling technology share prices, people who work for technology companies have discovered that you need cash, not options, to pay the grocery bills. In this more hostile environment companies like Enron and WorldCom were forced to the conclusion that the only way to produce the numbers the markets required was to invent them.

The danger now is of imploding corporations which disguise the continual erosion of their core business by consolidation and acquisition. Such companies react to each disappointing earnings report by further cost cuts and job reductions. They stave off the demands of their predatory investors by slicing further into muscle and bone.

But many investors now realise that few companies can generate sustainable double digit growth in earnings. The better alternative is a return to a more balanced conception of the nature of business. A world in which senior executives earn salaries. Great businesses – like Merck, Procter and Gamble, Shell and Marks and Spencer – were not built in the three to five year timescale that the consultants who devise management incentives describe as the long-term. The massive shareholder value these businesses generated was a by-product of their competitive strengths, not the object of the business itself: and for that reason was sustainable for long enough to deliver our pensions. Henry Ford – no mean creator of shareholder value – wrote that a business run only for profit would die because it had no long-term reason to exist. He might have been talking about Enron and WorldCom.

*25 November 1998*                                              *Copenhagen*

*Dear Linda,*

*Greetings from Copenhagen. It is 8.30 in the morning and I am
sitting in my room on the 34th floor of the Hotel Scandinavia. The
sky is blue and clear and views over the old city and across the
Kattegat to Sweden are stunning. Below, the traffic is moving
smoothly along the Amager Boulevard, the town's main traffic artery.*

*We are here to discuss the crisis facing the European social model.
The crisis is not immediately evident. From the moment of arrival at
Kastrup Airport, you are overwhelmed by a sense that Denmark is
efficient, rich and comfortable.*

*There is no sign of the economic and social tension evident when
you arrive at Kinshasa, Bangkok – or indeed New York. Both the
natural and the urban environments are enviable. The quality of
public services, particularly education, is exceptional. By any criteria,
Denmark is a pleasant place to live. True, the language is ridiculous.
But it is reassuring that the taxi driver speaks English, which is
rarely true in New York. And the facts and figures support these
superficial impressions. In 1996, incomes per head in Denmark were
around 20% higher than in the United States (the rise in the dollar
since then will have reduced this differential).*

*Still, we must get down to work and discuss the crisis. Taxes in
Denmark are nearly 60% of national income, the highest figure of
any country in the world. The labour market is heavily regulated.
Even in the private sector, over 90% of the work force is in trades
unions, which work closely together with employers and government
in one of the most corporatist of European economies. It is well*

*known that this combination of policies and institutions is restricting growth, stunting innovation and damaging employment.*

*These things are well known, but what is well known is not always true. The Danish economy did experience a difficult phase in the 1980s. During the 'blue period' – a decade of Conservative government – there was some restructuring and reform. But since the Social Democrats returned to power in 1993, Denmark has grown at the same rate as the United States, and well ahead of the world average.*

*But what is most well known is the devastating effect of the European social model on employment and unemployment. And unemployment is indeed higher in Denmark than in the United States. The gap narrows when you adopt the standardised basis created by the OECD: 6·0% in 1996 as against 5·4% in America. However the OECD calculations do not adjust for differences in the prison population, presumably because prisoners are not actively seeking work. Since there are 1·7 million people in jail in the United States, and only just over 3000 in Denmark, this is important.*

*If we add the proportion of the population incarcerated to the proportion unemployed, 6·6% of Americans were out of work in 1996 and 6·1% of Danes. There is a simple explanation for the difference* in unemployment. Young men who in Denmark are at home watching television and desultorily looking for employment are in jail in the United States and therefore out of the unemployment statistics. Since there is much less crime in Denmark than in America, it is not clear that the Danes have got it wrong.

But there is a strong feeling on the part of the Danes that they have indeed got it wrong, which is why we are all at this conference. Whether or not there is indeed a crisis in the European social model itself, there is certainly a crisis of confidence in the European social model. For many of those who attend meetings like this one, the existence of the problem is self-evident and only the means of tackling it needs to be discussed. They tell us that the era of the high-spending state, in which business is governed by both explicit and consensual regulation, is over. And that the day of the stakeholder company, embedded in the local community, is at an end. The European social model is at best a transitional form of capitalism, a staging post on the route to a full market economy.

And yet the undeniable fact is that if you are looking for the world's most successful economies, "small West European state" is more or less the best indicator you can find. Denmark ranks along with Norway, Switzerland, Austria, Luxembourg in any list of countries with high living standards, material and otherwise. And all these countries have other common characteristics. High, almost stifling levels of social cohesion and interlocking networks of corporations, employers and workers' organisations, and the state: the principal features of the supposedly defunct European social model.

These examples attract little serious attention. The shelves of the Saïd Business School library groan with volumes about Chaibol and Keiretsu. The books on China stretch the length of the Great Wall. But you will look in vain for titles like Great Entrepreneurs of Norway. The Coming Economic Powerhouse – Denmark, Iceland – Europe's Tiger Economy. These weaknesses in our library are not because we have not bought the books. They are not there because no-one has written them.

*When our students go on study trips they do not fly to Luxembourg or Finland. And when the international business elite meets in Davos, it appreciates Switzerland for its snow, sun and scenery, not as the world's most successful economy.*

*Perhaps some rethinking is in order. The Danes are anxious to participate in fashionable discussion of the crisis facing the European social model. There is a deep-seated angst in the Danish character. This is the country of Hamlet, Hans Christian Andersen, and Carlsberg Special lager. Danes worry about whether they deserve their good fortune, and are fearful that it might not continue. But beneath it all there is a quiet self-satisfaction. They know that their system works. And they do not need lectures about their crisis. It is time to go back to London.*

*John*

# A trip to the *marché municipal*

28 AUGUST 2003

It is a pleasant excursion to pick up some produce in Menton's *marché municipal* and browse the FT over an espresso in the Place Clemenceau. It was there that I read Robert Gordon's article (*Financial Times*, 20 August 2003) on the need to reduce the productivity gap between American and European retailers.

The little newsagent sells not only the FT and the usual run of French newspapers but also *The Wall Street Journal, Il Sole, El Pais*

and *Die Zeit.* There is certainly scope there for rationalisation and economies of scale. And the productivity of that espresso! So much coffee, so much energy, for such a small output of liquid.

And then there is the *marché municipal* itself, a striking but not beautiful 1902 building of 10,000 square feet. It contains about 50 stalls, all selling fresh foodstuffs. There are competing fruit, vegetable and cheese shops and at this time of year tourists are photographing the mouth-watering displays. The queue at the bread stall always spills out on to the street because many breads are sold by weight. There is a specialist potato place, where the vendor will advise you what is in season and which variety is most suitable for a boulangère.

The market is a tourist attraction; but it is not primarily a tourist attraction. Most shoppers are local residents. There will still be a queue to buy bread in November, and there will be a different range of potatoes. There are similar markets all over France.

French retailing is constrained by regulations on land use, opening hours and even the products that may be sold. France was one of the first countries to develop out-of-town stores and some of the companies that pioneered these developments, such as Carrefour, are innovative retailers in a global marketplace. Since then, there has been intensive lobbying by smaller merchants. It is almost impossible today to create new shopping centres on greenfield sites. But these self-serving arguments have been successful, not because their proponents made donations to political action committees, but because many French people are sympathetic to the cause. They fear the *marché municipal* might disappear.

I doubt if there is much justification for such concern. There are three supermarkets within a quarter of a mile of the market, which stock the same categories of goods, mostly of lower quality and at lower prices. On the outskirts of town is a much larger store with extensive parking. A 20-minute drive will take you to a Carrefour with more than 100,000 square feet of retail space and a US-style mall. In the face of this competition, the *marché municipal* and another daily market a mile away seem to be doing fine. All the stalls are taken and there are usually some informal booths outside where local people sell home-grown fruit and vegetables.

An economist, it is said, knows the price of everything and the value of nothing. But this is unfair; most economists would agree that value depends not only on price but also on quality – and that the quality of retailing is enhanced by a range of outlets and by diversity of product range, congenial surroundings and knowledgeable salespeople.

Nevertheless, such analysis is not what economists do. Productivity data show that the gap between Britain and the US is particularly large in financial services and in retailing. But these are industries in which output is poorly measured and British companies are successful in international competition. So we should look at what lies behind the figures before we draw conclusions.

National accounts measure not retail output but the volume of retailed goods. A dollar of sales is treated similarly whether it is made in Bloomingdales or Wal-Mart, in *haute couture* salon or the *marché municipal*. Higher productivity simply means less retail input per dollar of sales, so the conclusion that French productivity is lower is both obvious and meaningless. We take visitors to the *marché* because it is fun. I suspect that if you tried to photograph the displays in a Wal-Mart store you would be asked to leave, but that problem is not often encountered.

# An economist's tale: Amer and Eur

12 DECEMBER 1997

 Near my Oxford office is a pub called the Eagle and Child. J. R. Tolkien, author of *The Lord of the Rings*, would meet there with the Inklings, a group of literary dons. Tolkien was not the only member to turn his talents to allegorical fantasies: C.S. Lewis, author of *The Lion, the Witch and the Wardrobe*, was another Inkling. And I recently stumbled across a beer-stained manuscript written by a little-known business economist who was a member of their group.

His fantasy told of two islands, called respectively Amer and Eur. In Amer, the prevalent culture was strongly individualistic. People co-operated with each other, but they tended to do so on the basis of carefully drafted contracts and well designed systems of rules. Amerans viewed their constitution with almost reverential authority, and turned quickly to their lawyers in the event of accident or dispute.

Eur was a much more consensual society. Few of the conventions which governed business behaviour were written down: co-operation tended to be instinctive. Risks and information were to be shared, rather than managed strategically. Individual misfortunes were immediately matters of social concern.

Both Amer and Eur were very successful economically, but in different ways. Amer was a wonderfully innovative society, reflecting its emphasis on individual initiative and readiness to experiment. Eur was better at producing the kind of high quality manufactured goods which demanded commitment from the workforce and trust between firms. Amer firms were managed aggressively for the benefit of their owners (or the people who managed them). Eur firms were more conservative, with an emphasis on long-term organic growth. Amer companies were quick to seize new market opportunities: Eur firms were more inclined to invest in the evolution of their business and attached special importance to developing the skills of their workforce. Amer firms treated their workers instrumentally: Eur firms saw the employment relationship as a long-term commitment. These different competitive strengths worked to the benefit of both. Eur benefited from Amer innovation, while Euron products were widely admired in Amer.

There was some sort of dispute between Amer and Eur. (The details of this seemed to have been written and rewritten many times and I could not make them out). But following that dispute, a group of Amer political philosophers and economists, with attendant lawyers and merchant bankers, arrived on Eur shores to re-educate the population in the Amer values of liberal individualism.

At first, this didn't make a great deal of difference to the way the Eur economy worked. What had previously been described as social insurance was now reformulated in terms of welfare rights. What were once generally understood conventions about business behaviour were now defined and prescribed as state regulations. People carried on behaving in the same ways, they just talked about them differently.

But over time, the new rhetoric started to have its influence. Welfare rights conveyed little in the way of corresponding obligations. That made them increasingly expensive, while at the same time the majority of the Eur population, which had no need of them, became resentful of this cost. The social solidarity which had provided the initial basis of the welfare system started to erode.

And an advantage of business regulation based on consent was that it constantly and often imperceptibly adapted to changing economic conditions. Formal, legalistic regulation did not. Moreover, such regulation necessarily applied to all firms whether they could afford the costs of these obligations or not. Whenever change was proposed, interest groups gathered together to resist.

Practices which had formerly been helpful in making the Eur economy work increasingly became impediments to its progress.

All this eroded the self confidence of Eur business and Eur politicians. They worried about the road ahead. The visiting Amer philosophers – who had by now trained many Eurons in their systems of thought – were in no doubt about the answer. The problem with Eur was that it was still not Amer enough. If only Eur would roll back its welfare systems and dismantle its regulations, Eur could be as prosperous as Amer.

But not all Eurons were convinced. Many of them, of course, were simply defending what they had been encouraged to think of as their entitlements: they were underworked employees of state industries, or managers of companies failing to meet the challenge of world markets. Yet others were more thoughtful. They pointed out that incomes were as high in Eur as in Amer, which did not suggest that only the Amer model worked. They noted that many more Amerans enjoyed life in Eur than the other way round. They argued that Eur was unlikely to be more successful at being Amer than Amer was itself.

They asked whether is was not possible that many of the old Eur ways were the best – for Eur if not necessarily for Amer. They shared with the Amer ideologues a desire to restructure the welfare system. But they wanted to replace it with a structure that gave back responsibility for social insurance to firms, communities and new public-private partnerships. They also wanted to reduce state regulation in product and labour markets. But to do so on the basis that most of the objectives of that regulation, for consumer and worker protection, would be adopted by companies themselves.

Some of those who sympathised with this perspective also believed that the traditional Eur values could not be sustained in a world in which Amerans, and those who had acquired single capital market Amer values, dominated the single capital market which had come to embrace both islands. Perhaps they were right, perhaps wrong. The manuscript ends at this point.

# The political business cycle

30 MAY 2001

I recently came across an essay that I wrote as an undergraduate in the 1960s. My politics professor had asked me to tackle the thesis that the incumbent government would almost always be re-elected because it could manage the economy to create a pre-election boom. Then, as now, the view that economics drove politics dominated almost every discussion of political strategy.

The argument relied on three propositions. First, that the main influence on voting behaviour is the amount of money in the voter's pocket. Second, that the main concern of politicians is to secure re-election, and that this concern is the basis of their economic policies. Third, that governments actually have enough control over the economy to achieve their goals.

With the collapse of the Keynesian consensus since the 1960s, everyone is now more sceptical about the last of these claims. And since I wrote that essay, evidence has continued to accumulate that the first two propositions are also doubtful.

Do voters re-elect governments when the economy is doing well? The belief that governments would ensure economic growth and with it their own survival was a product of the 1950s, when – mostly right-wing – governments around the world had

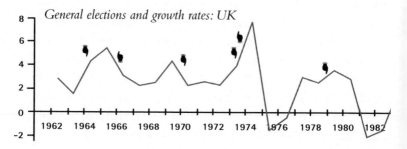

*General elections and growth rates: UK*

presided over rapid expansion and been resoundingly voted back
into office. In Britain, the achievement of Harold Macmillan in
1959 set the tone. His government told voters that they had never
had it so good and knocked twopence off the price of a pint of
beer just before the election.

But even in the 1960s, there were reasons to doubt that the
economy was the decisive issue. The Conservatives should have
won in 1964 (when the economy was booming and Sir Alec
Douglas-Home led his party to defeat), and Labour should have
lost in 1966 (when Harold Wilson was in charge of a rapidly
deteriorating economic scene). If you focus simply on the growth
rate in the economy, the best elections to have fought were those
of 1964, 1987 and 1997 (yet the government lost two out of three)
and the worst were those of 1966, 1974 and 1992 (yet the government won two out of the three).

Perhaps voters take a longer-term view, and assess performance
over the life of a parliament. If they do, they will find little difference in the outcomes of the parliaments of the last fifty years. Still,
the electorate should have been grateful to Edward Heath in 1974
(they were not) and to Margaret Thatcher in 1987 (they were).
And they should have punished James Callaghan in 1979 (they
did) and John Major in 1992 (they did not). If there is a relationship between economic performance and the results of British
parliamentary elections, it is not an obvious one.

The economy seems to have more of an influence in the United
States. Gerald Ford in 1976 and George Bush Sr in 1992 stood

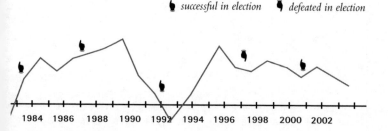

*successful in election*   *defeated in election*

1984  1986  1988  1990  1992  1994  1996  1998  2000  2002

before unfavourable economic backgrounds – and both lost. The most advantageous conditions were faced by Lyndon Johnson in 1964, Richard Nixon in 1972, Ronald Reagan in 1984, and Bill Clinton in 1996 – and each secured re-election. Al Gore should have won in 2000. Perhaps he did.

People who are cynical about election campaigns may find it surprising that politicians do not seem to manage the economy with their eye on re-election. But that is the conclusion of the most careful analysis of the relationship between economics and elections. Alesina and Roubini test two alternative hypotheses of political behaviour – the partisan and the opportunistic. The former theory assumes that the main influence on the actions of politicians is their declared views. The latter theory supposes that whatever they say, they will do whatever is needed to secure re-election.

The opportunistic theory suggests that business cycles will broadly coincide with electoral cycles. The partisan theory takes a different view of the relationship between politics and the economy. Left wing governments expand the economy in their first years in office and then, finding these policies mostly unsuccessful, retrench. Right wing governments contract the economy at the beginning of their term and then, also finding these policies unsuccessful, expand.

New Labour since 1997, and the Clinton administration in the US, are exceptional in not having followed these conventional partisan policies (and this may account for their success). But the model describes the Thatcher years, the Mitterand years, and the

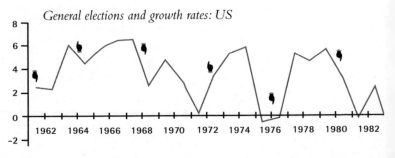

*General elections and growth rates: US*

recent changes of political control in continental Europe.

One implication of the partisan theory is that the economy is more likely to be booming when the election is called if there is a right wing government than a left wing government. Historically, this has been true. But if the thesis of cynical politicians and cynical voters were correct that would mean right wing governments would secure re-election more often than left wing ones. Mostly, they do not. If Labour wins on June 7, Conservatives, Labour and Republicans will each have won re-election three times since 1960 and Democrats twice. The Democrat score would have been three if Gore had taken Florida.

The theory of cynical, self-interested politicians manipulating cynical, self-interested voters is exaggerated. In the statistical analysis which Alesina and Roubini undertake, the partisan theory wins out clearly over the opportunistic theory. If econometrics does not lie, nor do politicians. The best explanation of their behaviour is that, for better or worse, they mean what they say. And the best explanation of voters' behaviour is that they make their minds up on the basis of the issues and the competence of governments. It is wise to be cynical about politics, but possible to be too cynical. As my professor was.

---

A general election was held in Britain on 7 June 2001 and Tony Blair's Labour Party was returned with a large, almost unchanged majority. The analysis of Alesina and Roubini can be found in *Political Cycles and the Macroeconomy*, MIT Press, 1977.

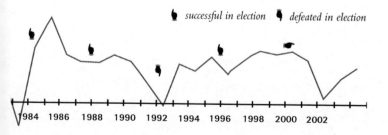

successful in election    defeated in election

1984   1986   1988   1990   1992   1994   1996   1998   2000   2002

# Economic policy

The central theme of 'The Truth about Markets' (p176)
is that markets function because, and only because, they
are embedded in a social, political and cutlural context.
In this environment, the important issues of economic
policy concern the ways in which government and
society influence the functioning of economic systems.
These are the questions discussed in this section. The
essays here cover both broad topics of the nature of
ownership and property rights and more specific problems
of the form of regulation and the nature of copyright.

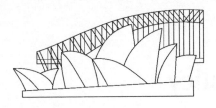

19 September 2001                                    Sydney

Dear Linda,

Greetings from Sydney. I am sitting in a waterfront restaurant with stunning views of the Harbour Bridge and the Opera House. Perusing the menu, I am puzzled by the fish.

It is twenty years since I first came to Australia. Its cuisine was then desperate and dull. The trademarks of the Australian kitchen were the meat pie and the oversized, overcooked steak.

Immigration from Southern Europe and Asia has changed all that. Sydney and Melbourne are now amongst the most interesting cities in which to eat. Yet there is still one curious feature of an Australian menu. The European visitor will find the same meats — beef, lamb, pork and chicken — as at home. And the fish are as good as any you will encounter in a French or English restaurant. But they are quite different fish. The highlights of this menu are barramundi, blue eye and King George whiting. In the suburbs of Australian cities there are fish and chip shops just like those you find in England— except that you'll find shark inside the batter, not cod.

It is easier to keep track of animals than fish. When European immigrants arrived in Australia, they brought familiar and useful animals — cows and sheep for food, horses for transport, cats and dogs as domestic pets. They didn't bring cod or sole because these creatures would have swum off into the Pacific Ocean.

Migrants did, however, bring trout and carp (but not many people like carp, and today they are a pest). They tried to introduce salmon, which return to their river of origin. But they did not realise that Atlantic salmon take to sea in search of Greenland fishing grounds: transported salmon were unable to find Greenland. Only when fish

HE JUST DIDN'T THINK IT THROUGH – FREE-RANGE FISH FARMING WAS NEVER GOING TO WORK

ROGER BEALE

*farming was developed did Tasmanian production allow salmon to make a regular appearance on Australian menus.*

*That explains the fish. But what of the meats? Why were they exported from Europe to Australia, but not from Australia to Europe? Australian farmers graze sheep and cows, but no European farmers breed kangaroos. This is what the anthropologist Jared Diamond described as 'Yali's question' when a New Guinean posed it for him – 'Why did you bring cargo to us, not us to you?' and Diamond devoted a remarkable book to unravelling the answer.*

*The simplest explanation is that Europeans imposed their culture on Australia but Australians did not impose theirs on Europe, except in London's Earl's Court. But that does not seem to be enough. Australians of English origin learned to drink their beer cold when they understood that was what the climate required. And even if they pined for lemon sole and battered cod, they quickly learnt to enjoy barramundi. Europeans were very ready to bring useful species from Australia. The mimosa which brightens southern France in February* was imported because it is beautiful and grows even better on the Tanneron massif than on its native soil.

So why were there many more plants and animals in Europe that had economic value in Australia than plants and animals in Australia which had economic value in Europe? Europeans may simply have been luckier than Australians in the range of plants and animals available to them. You really don't want to be a kangaroo farmer. Kangaroos are hard to keep penned in and their meat is not all that pleasant anyway.

But the docile cow that helpfully saunters to the milking parlour and sports succulent steaks at its rear end is not an animal which was ever found in the wild. Nor − whatever opponents of genetically modified crops may believe − is the wheat which goes into their organic bread a natural product. These strains are the product of thousands of years of domestication. The contented cow is the descendant of an animal every bit as unruly as the kangaroo. And its bovine ancestors probably could not match the flavour of a Charolais or Aberdeen Angus. Our human ancestors bred for flavour as well as convenience.

Modern agriculture was invented in Mesopotamia, in response to population pressures which made nomadic existence increasingly difficult. Knowledge of agriculture was transmitted to Europe along land corridors. Aboriginal Australians were cut off by sea from Europe and Asia. They lived in a vast country. So they neither discovered nor learnt of agriculture until the arrival of Captain Cook. And Cook's migrant successors brought animals and crops designed for economic efficiency − species that are cheap to rear and good to eat.

It might seem from this history that economic development is largely a matter of chance. And certainly chance has had large effects. The differences in the habits of cows and cod, the accident that certain grasses were found on the banks of the Euphrates but not the Murray River, the topography that placed a sea between China and Australia but not between Mesopotamia and Europe, have all strongly influenced economic history.

*Yet the larger lesson is that economic development is the product of the co-evolution of technology, the physical and social environment, and economic institutions. Historic differences in these interactions are the main source of the economic differences we observe today. That is why there is, and can be, no universal development model.*

*It is surprising how much you can learn while waiting for your host to arrive in a Sydney restaurant. Wish you were here – or he was.*

*John*

---

Jared Diamond's *Guns, Germs and Steel*, Vintage, (1998), is a sweeping survey of economic development over ten thousand years.

# A fetish for manufacturing

13 JUNE 1997

In 1980 I wrote an article which explained why contraction of manufacturing industry was an inevitable consequence of the growth of British North Sea oil production. This was my first encounter with manufacturing fetishists. The article proved to be very controversial. (It was, incidentally, right.) Few critics focused on weaknesses in the argument. They claimed instead that what I was saying ought not to be true or, if it was true, ought not to be said.

"Surely you don't think that an economy can survive on hairdressing and hamburger bars." No, I didn't; any more than I thought it could survive on steel and automobile production. But this was not really the point. I started to understand that for many people the role of manufacturing industry was an emotional issue rather than an economic one.

The origins of manufacturing fetishism might be better explored by a psychologist or an anthropologist than an economist, but let me try. Thousands of years ago, man hunted, fished and made primitive implements. If he was good at these things, his wife and children prospered; if not, they died. From these days, we have inherited the notion of a hierarchy of needs – food and shelter ahead of chartered accountancy and cosmetic surgery. With the hierarchy of needs comes a hierarchy of importance of economic activities – agriculture, primary resources and basic manufacturing come before hairdressing and television programming.

But these categorisations ceased to have economic relevance once technology and knowledge advanced enough for it to be unnecessary to hunt and fish all day in order to get enough to eat

– a state of affairs that was reached many years ago. Once primitive tribes had sufficient food, they started to add discretionary activities to their basic needs.

The services introduced then remain representative of the services we buy today. The priest who warded off evil; the bureaucrat ruled over the tribe; the repair man sharpened knives; and eventually the insurance agent organised a scheme of mutual support for unlucky villagers whose cow died or whose house burnt down. With the rise of a market economy came Adam Smith's division of labour. Specialist tasks were assigned to those best qualified to fulfil them.

As Smith noted, the division of labour was limited by the extent of the market, and the growth in the geographical scope of markets has steadily increased the division of labour. But even in the early stages of discretionary expenditure, the rewards of different activities were detached from their position in the hierarchy of needs. You only got paid for producing goods that people wanted, but it soon became apparent that insurance and priestly services were among the things they did want. Given that what you produced was wanted, earnings reflected the availability or scarcity of the talents needed to produce them, and your position in the power structure of the tribe. The first explains why the insurance and repair men did well, and the second accounted for the prosperity of the bureaucrat and the priest.

Those who are lucky enough to have power or rare talents have often felt embarrassed to earn more than those who work to satisfy more essential needs. Often, they also enjoy occupations that are less arduous and more fun. The embarrassment is rarely very great, and seems to have diminished recently. But emphasising the importance we attach to these other more necessary, but less well-remunerated activities, is a means of assuaging such embarrassment. Still, this moralising provides no sound basis for economic policy or industrial strategy.

A quite different argument for the special role of manufacturing emphasises that manufactured goods, unlike services, are sold to foreigners. Of course, many services are exported and many manufactures are not, but there is some truth in the stereotype.

But the real weakness in this argument points the way to the correct answer to the valuation of different activities. If what matters is the tradeability of output, then why draw the line around the nation state? Why not draw it more broadly, or more narrowly? Neither the City of London, nor a steel works, could survive on its own; you cannot drink derivatives or eat steel. The City and the steel mill survive and are valuable because, and only because, they can persuade people outside their boundaries to value their output. Their output is valuable, not because it can be sold to foreigners, but because it can be sold.

The economic significance of an activity is not measured by its place in an objective hierarchy of needs; it is measured by what someone, other than the producer, thinks it is worth. Almost all the lobbying which is done on behalf of allegedly important but neglected activities comes from producers who have failed to persuade other people to value what they do. The makers of high-cost manufactured goods which are already in excess supply, like steel and textiles. The producers of the films that people want to make but audiences do not want to go and see. Farmers who grow foodstuffs at twice the cost of obtaining them from more favoured parts of the world. People who have advanced techno-logical solutions to problems that do not exist.

Whatever industrial policy we are going to have, beware of any that is predicated on a consensus on which economic activities are more important than others. That judgement is always better left to the market.

---

The 1980 article co-authored with P J Forsyth, was 'The Economic Implications of North Sea Oil Revenues', *Fiscal Studies*, July 1980.

# Does foreign ownership matter?

20 DECEMBER 1996

Does it matter if all of Britain's electricity generating companies are owned by Americans? If all our major investment banks are subsidiaries of Continental European financial institutions? If the British owned car industry closes down and is replaced by one which is mostly owned by the Japanese? If we have to get our KitKats from the Swiss, our water from the French, and our beta blockers from the Germans?

The French government clearly thinks it is important that French businesses be French controlled. That is why it has recoiled from the prospect that its consumer electronics industry might fall into the hands of the Koreans, vetoing Daewoo's proposed purchase of this part of Thomson's business. Not a problem the British government has to worry about: the equivalent goods here have for years been made by firms called Sony, Hitachi and Samsung. We in Britain took a different view. Kuwaiti ownership of a 20% stake in British Petroleum was too much to bear: the Monopolies and Mergers Commission was horrified by the prospect that the Royal Bank of Scotland's head office might move to London, far less Hong Kong. But not any more.

Now it is costly to be xenophobic in economic matters. It is an undeniable, if depressing, fact that under British ownership automobile production and consumer electronics industries failed to meet the challenges of international competition. We did make things worse for ourselves by merging all our small weak competitors into a large weak competitor in the hope that one national champion would enjoy critical mass, global scope, and several other industrial policy clichés. But that is in the past.

Today, the only way we can have viable firms in cars and consumer electronics is to have Japanese ownership, management and design.

And if American companies want to buy our regulated utilities for more than they are worth, the difference is a net gain to UK plc. The world is full of regulated companies with more cash than knowledge of the markets they would like to enter, convinced that the grass must be greener somewhere else. What really ought to concern us is not when foreigners buy here, but when our own companies, suffering from the same misconceptions, believe that the regulatory climate will be more benign in Bangkok or Buenos Aires than it is in Birmingham.

So should we just let the market rip? I'm not so sure. An economy in which we are all employed as production workers for foreign companies, and then retire on well funded pensions we have financed by selling off the future earning streams of our companies to overseas investors, is certainly better than one in which there is little employment and no pensions. But in the long run our prosperity depends on the skills and capabilities of our firms and our workforce, and this rentier society is unlikely to develop these.

This brings us to the nub of the matter. Our national economic objective is to maximise the added value which is created in Britain. We can only add value by having skills and capabilities – in people or in firms – which are better than those of the companies and countries with whom we are in international competition. So we should welcome foreign ownership when it adds to British skills and capabilities. And we should deplore foreign ownership if it means that the development of these skills takes place somewhere else, or that the benefits of enhancing the value of British capabilities accrue to someone else.

So we should not be too disturbed by the fact that much of what is done in the City of London is done by firms with foreign parents. Ownership may have been transferred, but London is still where the value is added, and that means that the return from adding that value will be earned here. You only have to look at what people in the City are paid to see that this is true, and that the increasing involvement of foreign companies in London has led to bidding up of the earnings of people with specialist skills. More than that, the presence of so many foreign companies here actually helps to enhance these skills and emphasise the role of London as the centre where they are located.

But we should be more sceptical about those foreign direct investments which are the subject of enthusiastic ministerial announcements: creating, they tell us, thousands of jobs in depressed regions of the country. These companies have not come here to make British skills available to a wider market. They have been attracted by the top bidder in a subsidy competition among many regions of Europe and often among regions of the UK. This is a competition among areas all of which can offer equivalent – generally rather low – levels of resource and capability.

And we should be more sceptical still about allowing control of British industries to pass into foreign hands if that means either that future development of the strength of these industries will be driven from overseas, or that the benefits of enhancing these competitive strengths will be derived overseas. Whatever is said about globalisation of the world economy, most companies remain resolutely national at the most senior levels of operation, and their highest added value activities are biased towards their home country.

So we should think long and hard before allowing others to acquire our pharmaceutical or aerospace capabilities, even at extravagant prices. And it is good that our electricity industry should have access to American skills and expertise, but very undesirable that we should end up with no electricity distribution company headquartered here. As in so many other areas of economic activity, progress comes from diversity: and neither British laissez-faire, or French chauvinism, guarantee that result.

# The practice of regulation

28 APRIL 1999

Last week the Financial Services Authority published its first occasional paper, on The Economic Rationale of Financial Services Regulation. Gripping reading, at least for those for whom meetings of the Association of City Compliance Officers are the social highlights of the year. For the rest of us, it may be more fun to think about beards and the customs of Oxford Senior Common Rooms – and there are lessons there for the economic rationale of financial services regulation in both the barber's shop and the ivory towers.

It is not long since a French cultural anthropologist came to Oxford to help us understand the differences between the business environments in different countries. (We do not share the fashionable perception that the new international manager can operate in the same way wherever she finds herself). The anthropologist began by describing the rules for determining seniority in an American factory, rules which had been the subject of long negotiation between company and unions.

Seniority is based on date of joining the firm. If two or more employees arrive on the same date, their relative seniority is determined by the alphabetical order of their surnames. However if an employee changes his or her surname after (though not before) the date of joining, seniority will not be affected. If Miss Zybrowski marries Mr Aardvark and adopts his name, she gains nothing in terms of workplace rights. If her brother marries her sister-in-law, once more nothing is changed.

The audience laughed, as they were intended to, at the absurdity of all this. But we need to be careful when we laugh. In France,

there is certainly seniority, but it is not the product of any system of rules. It is more often the product of attendance at ENA or Ecole Polytechnique. Such networking interacts with the many conventions of French society which are well known to everyone among the French élite, though not to those who are outside it. What determines seniority is complex, changing, and incapable of being written down.

And then the Oxford contingent realised how little cause they had for laughter. The seniority rules the American company had adopted are exactly the rules that determine seniority in the Oxford common room. You will not find these principles set out anywhere, but woe betide the unwary newcomer who mistakenly sits in the Senior Fellow's chair at dessert: or the junior fellow who thinks she can ascend the ladder of seniority by changing her name. What the English listeners found absurd was not that such behaviour should exist, but that anyone would go to the trouble of writing the conventions down.

The exchange illustrated different approaches to rule-making, each consonant with the particular culture from which it emerged. You can seek definition, and insist on due process: but in doing so you create bureaucracy and lose flexibility. And you have to choose.

American regulation demonstrates one choice. If you thought American employers were free of burdensome rules, think again. Be sure you are aware of paragraph (g)(l)(i)(A) of the Occupational Safety and Health Administration's (OSHA) rules on respirators, which prohibits you from allowing respirators with tight-fitting facepieces to be worn by employees who have 'facial hair that comes between the sealing surface of the facepiece and the face'. Beards, in other words.

But also stubble. The OSHA did not adopt this regulation without careful research. It supported studies in which volunteers grew beards over an eight week period, submitting to regular tests of how well their respirators fitted. Following these experiments, it was able to conclude that "individuals with excessive facial hair, including stubble and wide sideburns, that interfere with the seal cannot expect to obtain as high a degree of respirator perform- ance as clean shaven individuals." So the administration promulgated rules referring to the size, curliness and texture of the beard.

British regulation of the same issues takes the opposite pole. A UK employer must engage in a risk assessment. "The purpose of the risk assessment is to help the employer determine what measures should be taken to comply with duties under the relevant statutory provisions." And that, essentially, is it. You are in breach of the regulations if you have failed to engage in the risk assessment or have not adopted appropriate measures in the light of it. The Health and Safety Executive will give you advice and encouragement. But what you do is up to you. Only beware of criminal penalties if you get it wrong.

The American structure tells you what you must do, the British system leaves responsibility with the employer. The American structure provides legal certainty, but at the cost of complexity, irrelevance and the stifling of any imagination or initiative. And that is the basic choice in financial services regulation. Should we prescribe general principles, and leave firms themselves to work out the basis of implementation: or offer detailed prescription as to how business should be conducted? Neither answer is universally right.

Go for specific regulation of behaviour when the objective and content of the rule are obvious, where it is reasonably easy to see whether or not the rule has been implemented, and where the content and purpose of the rule are unlikely to change much over time. So we need rules to say do not release too much smoke into the atmosphere, do not sell food that contains poisonous substances, keep client money separate from your own.

Go for general principles when the purposes of the rule are more complex, where its application requires business knowledge that the regulator cannot have, where observance is difficult to monitor, and where technology and markets imply that the rule book must change frequently. So we should leave it to those on the ground, or in the factory, to decide how much stubble is acceptable in the workplace and what is best advice, and what information should to be given to customers in the sale of financial services.

And never forget your obligations under the OHSA: use a long-handled tool to pick up items you drop into a confined space.

# An economist's tale: BE's dress code

12 JANUARY 1996

In 1996, Don Cruickshank who was then Director General of Oftel, responsible for the regulation of telecommunications in the UK, proposed that the licences of BT and other telecom companies should be modified to include a general prohibition on anti-competitive behaviour. This proposal was strongly resisted by BT. The company argued that practices which cause concern should be the subject of specific prohibition. Only in this way could the business have a clear understanding of what it was, and was not, permitted to do.

---

When British Everything was finally privatised, the company decided it was time to shake off the sloppy dress habits of the public sector. A directive went round telling senior employees that they should adopt suitable business dress.

The directive caused some resentment. Those who opposed it demanded greater clarity and certainty. When they went to the wardrobe in the morning, how could they know what would or would not represent suitable business dress? After advice from its legal and regulatory affairs department, the company agreed to promulgate a dress code. Senior male employees were expected to wear smart suits, shirts with collars, and ties.

It was not long before someone came to the office in a red suit. When criticised, he pointed to the terms of the dress code. The suit was undeniably smart: but it was the smartness of Stringfellows rather than the boardroom. So the dress code had to specify colour. Red was out, grey was in. Some blues were clearly acceptable. The Chairman's favourite suit was a fetching shade of navy. But bright blues could not be admitted. So how bright was bright? Research came up with the answer. Brightness is determined by how much light a fabric reflects. A machine could measure this, and one was soon installed in the reception area.

But ties posed a more intractable problem. Which colours and motifs were acceptable, which not. A clearance procedure seemed the best answer. Anyone who bought a new tie could submit it to the dress code department, which had 42 days to rule on whether or not it was suitable business dress. This determination was difficult, since the appropriateness of a tie might depend on the context. So decisions were rather conservative.

The resulting controversy raised the issue of an appeal mechanism. Of course all changes in the dress code had to be agreed by the main board. But discretion over ties had been delegated to the dress code department. The department was consequently judge and jury in implementing regulations it had itself devised, which violated natural justice. So a small group of senior directors, with an independent fashion adviser, would hear complaints from employees who felt their ties had been unreasonably rejected. Some of these directors were heard to mutter that this was not what they were paid large salaries for. But no-one knew what they were paid large salaries for anyway.

Yet there was the more general problem of changing fashion. It was not so long since every gentleman had gone to work in a wing collar and frock coat. Not only were other forms of dress now acceptable, but wing collars had probably ceased to be acceptable. Not the image of a modern company in the information age. The fashion designer Paul Smith agreed to chair a standing working party to advise the company on fashion trends.

The dress code soon extended to 50 impenetrable pages. Knowledge of its contents was confined to the dress code department, which by this time consisted of twenty people, mostly lawyers, the union representative, and a few cranks who enjoyed pointing out inconsistencies and anomalies in the code.

Eventually new managers came in, determined to sweep the dress code department away. They quickly realised there were two alternatives. One was to supply a uniform to all employees. Such central dictation represented an intolerable interference in personal affairs. The other was to sweep away the dress code and renew the instruction to wear suitable business dress. If anyone was in genuine doubt as to what constituted suitable business dress – and not many people were – they were advised to have a word with Don, selected for his sound judgement and extensive business experience. What Don said bound no-one, but to ignore his advice was injudicious and might prejudice advancement in the company.

---

The demand for clarity and certainty in regulation has great superficial plausibility, and it is because it is difficult to argue against clarity and certainty it is best to proceed by analogy. The world is rarely clear and certain, and if it seems so today it will have ceased to be so tomorrow. It is no more possible or sensible to give an exhaustive description of what constitutes anti-competitive behaviour than to define suitable business dress. When is it competitive and when is it predatory to charge a low price? Or different prices to different customers? In both cases, you can exemplify things that are, and illustrate things that are not. But you are trying to promote an attitude and a style of behaviour. For those who understand that, formal rules are irrelevant; for those who do not, they have little value.

The demand for clarity and certainty comes from two sources. From the naive, who do not realise that regulation which eliminated discretion would involve intrusion in every aspect of business life. And from those who are far from naive, and understand that the impracticality of what they seek would emasculate regulation through interminable legalism.

# Copyright and creativity

31 MARCH 1999

In common with Nana Mouskouri, Iron Maiden, Tom Jones und die Fantastischen Vier, I regard myself as a creative person, providing original material for the entertainment and edification of the citizens of the European Union. Unlike my fellow artists, who recently successfully petitioned the European Parliament under the banner of "artists for strong copyright", I think that the draft directive they commented on will damage, not help, our interests.

Like die Fantastischen Vier and other artists, my first concern is to propagate my ideas as widely as possible. My second concern is to get credit for these ideas. My third objective is to be well paid for them. So why is it that the proposed directive has at its heart the obligation to allow a right "to prohibit direct or indirect, temporary or permanent reproduction by any means and in any form", when prohibiting reproduction is exactly the opposite of what we creatives want to achieve? The answer is that the law of intellectual property has been hijacked by a group of producer interests which want to build commercial monopolies in books, journals, records and software on the back of their exclusive access to original talent.

Now I doubt if Iron Maiden had thought deeply about the future of the knowledge economy when their agent or publisher persuaded them to sign a petition headed 'take a stand for creativity, take a stand for copyright'. They were probably told that dissemination of their work depended on a strong publishing industry. There is some truth in this claim. But the interests of creative talent and its publishers are far from identical.

Publishers may tell us that the distribution of the songs of Iron Maiden, or of my nearly completed and nearly unreadable monograph, depend on their ability to protect their copyright. But there is little basis for this assertion. Iron Maiden is in the same position as Jane Austen and Charles Dickens, whose books are widely available despite the absence of copyright, because the demand for their output is large. And my monograph does not gain anything from copyright because the demand for it is small and in practice no-one is going to copy it. My problem is to find any publisher at all and if I succeed in that, I can be entirely certain that no-one else will bother to launch a competing diversion.

The proposed copyright directive attempts to protect rights holders, rather than creative people. The production of scholarly journals emphasises the distinction. When you submit an article to an academic journal, the publisher requires you to assign the copyright, and the rightsholder takes over from the author. The main producers of academic articles are universities, and the main users of academic articles are universities. The net effect of the system is that universities pay large sums to publishers for severely restricted rights to use the material they themselves have created. Indeed under the proposed directive, the only way to avoid paying for a copy of an article you yourself have written is to write it again.

It is difficult to fathom how this system represents 'a stand for creativity'. It is true that in its absence there would be fewer academic journals. But almost everyone I know in the university world thinks there are too many academic journals. Robert Maxwell led the exploitation of this system. He launched dozens of journals. Some were successful. They became the leading publications in their field, and all universities had to subscribe, whatever the cost. Most failed, and continued to publish second rate material. The result has been a proliferation of journals, many of them publishing only bad articles, to the profit of no-one but the publisher. And the growth in the range of outlets has reinforced the publish or perish culture, in which it is the number rather than the quality of academic publications which counts.

Such anomalies and distortions could be reduced if universities retained copyright in the work of their employees, rather than allowing them to give it away to publishers. If there is to be a copyright licensing agency it would surely be more sensible if universities licensed publishers to use the material produced in universities rather than – as at present – publishers licensing universities to use the material produced in universities.

Reforms of copyright should genuinely be aimed at fostering creativity. It is important to creative people – Iron Maiden, Jane Austen, and John Kay – that they should be able to insist that their work appears only in ways which respect the integrity of the original (this is described as the moral right of authors). It is important to creative people that they should be able to disseminate their work as widely as possible and in the ways that they think best. It is important to creative people that they should be rewarded for the work they do. The right of their publisher to prevent unauthorised reproduction – which is at the heart of the copyright directive – achieves these objects incidentally at best, and often conflicts with them.

The legal rules which govern the production and distribution of original materials really matter in a knowledge economy and an information age. We need to encourage the widest possible dissemination of new ideas and innovations and reward those who produce them in direct relation to the originality and economic importance of these ideas and innovations. A system of intellectual property that achieves this will be based, not on a legal analysis of rights, but an economic analysis of costs and benefits. The basic principle should be open reproduction for reasonable reward. One of the first things the new European Commission should do is rethink the copyright directive from scratch. And perhaps there might even be an advantage in having a professor of economics as its President.

Romano Prodi, President of the European Commission from 1999 to 2004, was formerly Prime Minister of Italy and Professor of Economics at the University of Bologna. My monograph, greatly improved, was published in 2003 as *The Truth about Markets*. Copyright in it remains with John Kay. Individual articles from *Everlasting Light Bulbs* may be freely reproduced for non-commercial purposes without specific permission provided the source is acknowledged.

# The case for the just price

9 JULY 1999

In the last two weeks, most people's attention has been focussed on whether Tim Henman could finally succeed at Wimbledon. For business economists, however, the interesting events were outside Centre Court. The All England Club took out injunctions to clear ticket touts from the streets of Wimbledon.

Ticket touting is an issue that sharply divides economists from the rest of the world. Touts have a bad reputation. The tout is the archetypal middleman. The ticket he sells is – if you are lucky – the same as the ticket he buys. He adds no value; he profits from being in the right place at the right time. And even if Henman is there, most people feel that Centre Court tickets ought not to be sold for £1000. Prices should be fair. Matthew Parris writes of his aunt 'who votes Conservative, takes the Daily Telegraph and regards socialism as the work of the devil' but for whom 'a fair price is what will secure a reasonable profit after paying employees a decent wage' (*Times*, 21 December 1992).

The professional economist views such popular disdain for enterprise with patronising and detached amusement. Being in the right place at the right time is one of the most valuable services in the market economy. He views the concept of the just price with ridicule. Aristotle and Thomas Aquinas may have approved it, but today they would fail their preliminary examinations in any good university. In the Thatcherite years *The Economist* magazine would regularly deliver a defence of touts. 'Burly policemen set upon groups of entrepreneurs; the crime of these young businessmen was to sell tickets for the well-known tournament at more than the price dictated by their monopoly supplier'. (1988) 'Scalpers are fighters for justice.' (1991).

And I owe the Parris quotation to Sir Samuel Brittan, for whom the absurdity of the views of Parris' aunt needs no elaboration. 'I have made a few soundings of my own among business journalists, who might be expected to have a higher degree of sophistication. But even here I find great resistance.'

Now the free market position has obvious force. I have a ticket for Wimbledon but, because I am poor and not very interested in tennis, would prefer £1000; you would willingly part with £1000 to be there on finals day. It is difficult to see why the police should devote time and energy to preventing this mutually beneficial exchange. We would not retain laws against burglary if people wanted to be burgled. The tout who brings us together is doing a service to you, to me and to economic efficiency.

I used to share these free market views, which is how I got through my economics exams: but now I am not so sure. Doubts first began to creep in during the property market recession a few years ago. We tried to let an office. The agent advised us to put it on the market at £27 per square foot. He told us it would be hard to rent. He was right. After a couple of months, no-one had even come to see it.

We walked into his office with the condescending smirk that is the badge of the professional economist. We believed in the laws of supply and demand, and if we could not let our property it was because the price was too high. We told him to reduce it to £22 per square foot. He shook his head, but we insisted.

Again, he was right. No-one came to see our building, and eventually we accepted the agent's advice and put the rent up again. Finally, a prospective tenant arrived and liked the building. We gave him a suitable rent-free period and other sweeteners and his company moved in. I am sure he prospered, even if he paid too much.

As I reflected on what had happened, I understood that the

agent's claim that £27 per square foot was a fair rent for the property was not the economic absurdity I had thought. Properties are complicated and idiosyncratic. Even elaborate descriptions tell you much less than you need to know. When we quoted a price, we were not just trying to bargain, we were saying that this was a £27 per square foot property.

And when we offered it at £22 per square foot, prospective takers did not think they were getting a bargain. Nor should they: economists would have told them that bargains are few and far between in an efficient market. Would-be tenants thought there was something wrong with our premises which was not revealed in the particulars. By cutting the price we had made our offer less attractive, not more. And the best strategy was the one the agent advised – waiting for someone for whom our property was exactly right.

Such strategies explain features of the property market which puzzle economists. Prices do not rise enough in booms, or fall enough in slumps to clear the market. Despite price fluctuations, shortages and gluts emerge. Price adjustments often take the form of sweeteners rather than variations in the headline rent. And estate agents quite properly hold to a concept of intrinsic value which is distinct from market price.

And the same is true in the employment market. If someone calls you and offers to work for 20% less than the going wage, you are less, not more, likely to give them an interview. And for good reason. They might be calling you to tell you that the supply of good candidates for this job now exceeds demand and the market price for the activity in question has just fallen. Or they might have been unsuccessful in obtaining employment elsewhere. You do not know which, it is costly for you to find out, and you are inclined to suspect the latter.

And that is why both employer and employee are wise to have in their mind some concept of the intrinsic value of a job. The notion of intrinsic value moves less rapidly than the market clearing price, which equates supply and demand. And so Matthew Parris' aunt is right to base her concept of intrinsic value on what will yield a decent, but not unconscionable, profit: and the All-England Club is not necessarily mistaken in insisting that the prices at which its tickets are sold do not vary with the fortunes of Tim Henman. Consumers are entirely rational to choose to buy more when they believe that prices are set fairly. In a market economy, prices exist to convey information, as well as to equate supply and demand. Aristotle, Aquinas, and our estate agent understood something that many professional economists do not.

---

Sir Samuel Brittan's comments are contained in Chapter 1 of his *Capitalism with a Human Face,* published in 1995 by Edward Elgar.

# The permanent way

14 JANUARY 2004

*A well-furnished office on the south bank of the Thames. A famous playwright is consulting an important theatre director*

FAMOUS PLAYWRIGHT: I've written this play about British rail privatisation.

IMPORTANT THEATRE DIRECTOR: It doesn't sound like a box office winner to me.

FAMOUS PLAYWRIGHT: Don't worry, they'll come down in droves from Islington and Hampstead to hiss the investment banker and jeer at the politicians. It's like a pantomime, but for grown-ups.

IMPORTANT THEATRE DIRECTOR: Well, you packed them in to boo Rupert Murdoch and laugh at bishops and judges. We'll give it a try. Only in the small auditorium, though.

*The theatre bar, during the interval. Enter four theatregoers in search of refreshment.*

1ST THEATRE GOER: So what do you think of the play?

HER COMPANION (AN OFF-DUTY ECONOMIST): I laughed at the self-serving city gents, and the smug Treasury official. There's truth in these stereotypes. But the play is caricature. Dickens not Shakespeare, and without the wit.

1ST THEATREGOER: The chief executive of Railtrack was more finely drawn.

OFF-DUTY ECONOMIST: Yes, you saw a man out of his depth.

BARMAN: These privatised industry bosses! People who joined the water board in 1969 and suddenly imagined themselves titans of international business.

3RD THEATREGOER, AT OTHER END OF BAR: I like the way modern art is so socially aware! It's exhilarating to see contemporary issues aired in such a probing manner.

4TH THEATREGOER: And not just in the theatre! Grayson Perry won the Turner Prize for painting disturbing images of family life on ceramic vases! And Bono uses popular music to raise awareness of world poverty!

BARMAN, CLEARING AWAY THEIR DRINKS: Pretentious rubbish. Don't tell me that transvestite potters exhibiting abducted children on vases reduces child abuse. Or that Bono has anything to say about world poverty, except that he's against it. Do you know anyone in favour of world poverty?

*The theatre restaurant, after the play: four diners are seated.*

1ST THEATREGOER: So what did go wrong with rail privatisation?

OFF-DUTY ECONOMIST: You heard the playwright: "What was foredoomed to fail, failed".

1ST THEATREGOER: Well, that was true in *Hamlet* and *Macbeth*. But somehow Shakespeare developed the theme better.

*Another table.*

3RD THEATREGOER: The famous playwright is so right! 'Nobody believes that by being angry, by expressing anger, anything changes, anything can change'. That's what's wrong today!

4TH THEATREGOER: And his work is focussed and pertinent! None of those thirty-five line soliloquies about 'to be or not to be'. Just, 'What's the ****ing point?' We need more blunt speaking like that.

BARMAN (NOW ACTING AS WAITER): These people confuse anger and emotion with social comment and economic analysis. Nothing does change because you express anger, nor should it. I'll take the other couple their food.

OFF-DUTY ECONOMIST: The play's explanation of privatisation's failure, apart from the general venality of its characters, is fragmentation. The division of responsibility between operating companies and the network business. But I'm not convinced.

1ST THEATREGOER: Why not?

OFF-DUTY ECONOMIST: Most processes in a modern economy are similarly fragmented.

WAITER: Dead right. The person who is serving your steak didn't butcher the cow, and I can pour the wine even though someone else trampled the grapes.

OFF-DUTY ECONOMIST: The ability to coordinate disparate functions is one of the strengths of market economies.

1ST THEATREGOER: So what did go wrong?

OFF-DUTY ECONOMIST: The nature of legitimate authority is a central theme of Shakespeare's, and a key issue here.

WAITER: What he means is that whatever the arguments for privatisation, the public was not persuaded that the restructuring made sense, or that Railtrack should be a private company.

OFF-DUTY ECONOMIST: This absence of popular consent for the process didn't matter so long as things worked reasonably well. But as soon as they went wrong, press and public turned on those who had failed to establish legitimate basis for their power. Railtrack panicked, and destroyed itself. Well explored, the story has all the structure of a Shakespearean tragedy.

*An office, two men seated.*

FAMOUS PLAYWRIGHT: I have this new piece, *Over the Rainbow*, about US economic policy.

IMPORTANT THEATRE DIRECTOR: I think we're booked out for a revival of *Guys and Dolls.*

---

David Hare's play, *The Permanent Way*, opened at the Cottesloe Theatre on January 13 2004.

British Rail was privatised in the mid 1990s, with services provided by train operating companies while a different company, Railtrack, owned and maintained the tracks. Railtrack went into administration in October 2001 and the rail infrastructure was effectively renationalised under a new entity, Network Rail.

# In defence of economics

The social life of the economist is not an easy one. In line with the public view that economics is about what is going to happen to interest rates, people expect that your main interest is in forecasting. They expect you to be boring, opinionated, and mostly wrong. The essays in this section are a response to these standard criticisms of economists: ending with comments on the current state of economics as a profession, through advice to a niece.

# Plain English

2 MARCH 1998

Professor Richard Gregory, Fellow of the Royal Society, is an angry man. He has been awarded a golden bull for gobbledegook by the Plain English Campaign. What Professor Gregory (or actually one of his contributors) wrote, in the *Oxford Companion to the Mind*, was that 'novel peptides from the brain with actions related to functions such as pain, analgesia, sleep etc. are being discovered at an increasing rate' and he went on to explain that the importance of peptides in brain function was based on the ability to relay messages selectively. Got that?

Professor Gregory has a point. There is an important distinction to be drawn between the jargon that professionals use to communicate concisely with each other, and jargon which charlatans use to disguise the vacuity of what they are saying. Unfortunately, Professor Gregory immediately shot himself in the foot by explaining that such statements were necessary 'for the purposes of interfacing with the wider literature'. I think what he meant was they would help you read other books.

Every serious subject has jargon. Economists need to know about heteroscedasticity. The word is almost impossible to pronounce, and impossible to use in front of a class without everyone bursting out into laughter. Most spell-check programmes reject it, and offer improbable or embarrassing alternatives.

Yet heteroscedasticity is an important concept. When we measure things, we make mistakes. A measurement process is heteroscedastic when the mistakes are related to the size of the thing you measure. Judging distance by eye is heteroscedastic. A metre is a big error if you are estimating the size of your living room for the carpet fitter, but if you were only a metre out in guessing the length of your street, you would think you had done pretty well. But measuring with a rod is probably homoscedastic. Your measurements will still be slightly inaccurate but the inaccuracy will not be much larger in judging large distances than small. That is why it makes sense to judge small distances for yourself but to rely on the Ordnance Survey if you want to know the length of the journey from London to Birmingham.

So when economists use data, it is often important to know whether or not the process by which they were complied is heteroscedastic. This term has the characteristics of necessary jargon. Economists, who are in the business of collecting unreliable data, need to worry about whether their sources are heteroscedastic: ordinary people do not. The unfortunate term conveys an immediate meaning to those who have been educated in econometrics more concisely than the elaborate, but still imperfect, explanation above.

People who disparage this sort of jargon simply betray their own ignorance, and it is sad that the Plain English Campaign, which serves a good cause, has fallen into this trap. Some people think that what they do not understand is not worth knowing. When critics laughed at Gordon Brown for talking about post neo-classical endogenous growth theory, the laugh was on them. Endogenous means, roughly, that growth was generated by internal rather than external factors: neo-classical, roughly, that the use of resources corresponded to what would have happened in competitive markets. It is important to know whether growth of the Asian tiger economies was endogenous, and an answer might well help one understand the future of these economies and give advice to others. While one would probably not want to use this language when delivering an inspirational message to a constituency Labour party, we ought to be glad that we have a Chancellor who understands these terms instead of one who finds matchsticks a useful way of keeping accounts.

All sciences and professions have their own jargon. They benefit from the immediate clarity of meaning to other insiders which legitimises the use of terms such as heteroscedastic or endogenous, hypertension or contingent liability, neutrino or *ex parte* injunction. It doesn't matter that most people don't understand these terms. All of them have precise meanings which are familiar to those with appropriate training.

But this does not mean that the creation of jargon establishes a science. Much bad sociology or philosophy has this character. And management suffers even more. There is an obvious difference between technical terms such as hypertension or neutrino and words like shoddipush or horse blanket – to take two prize examples from the FT's business jargon competition – whose meaning is known only to those who have just made them up, and not necessarily even to them. Some consultants claim copyright for their manufactured terminology. Since the law refuses to allow copyright in an idea, if there was anything worthwhile in their analysis others can pinch it with impunity: all these people can protect is their verbiage.

At best, spurious jargon leads to the convoluted expression of ideas which could be simply conveyed in everyday language – as in 'interfacing with the wider literature'. At worst, it conceals essential confusion or vacuity of thought. But, in seeing through this pretension, we should not forget that jargon sometimes has its place.

---

In 1997 and 1998 the Financial Times held a competition in which readers were invited to select the worst examples of business jargon. The horse blanket came from Gemini consulting and shoddipush – the deadly syndrome that whiteants most businesses – was featured in the advertisement for John Wareham's 1 day MBA (sic).

# Economics in the movies

14 APRIL 1999

The Bodleian Library shuts for the week after Easter. So instead of burrowing through its dusty books and periodicals, I was forced to rummage among the old videos at home. Still, there is plenty to be learnt there about business and economics.

Not, however, from *Wall Street*, in which Gordon Gekko famously pronounced that greed was good. Or from *The Bonfire of the Vanities* – Hollywood was unable to accept the essentially desolate nature of Tom Wolfe's critique of modern New York, and messed up the story by appointing a wise old black judge to ensure a happy ending for everyone involved.

I found more of interest in James Dean's cult movie of the 1950s, *Rebel Without a Cause*. The highlight of the film is a game called chicken. Dean and his rival each drive a car towards a cliff. You win the game by jumping from the car later than the other player, but still in time to avoiding falling over the cliff.

Chicken is a familiar business situation. If you blink first, you lose. But if neither of you blinks, you lose still more. Every negotiation has elements of chicken about it. Still, the Dean version of the game is a difficult one to analyse. To learn about the mathematics of movies, it is easier to start with the simpler version of chicken that you find in *Stand by Me*.

Here, the two protagonists each drive a car towards the other, on a road wide enough to accommodate only one vehicle. You win the game if you drive straight ahead while your rival swerves. If you both swerve, you both look foolish. And if neither swerves, disaster lies ahead. This too is a common business problem. A market opportunity is profitable if one firm goes for it, but if many firms try all will lose money. London financial services demonstrated a classic chicken game. After deregulation in 1986 twenty-eight firms attempted market making in gilts, for example, and so long as that number tried none could possibly make money. Only when enough had jumped, or swerved, might profits be earned.

There are several surprising lessons from chicken games. One is that – as was true in financial services in London – it is possible to lose far more than any potential gain could ever have justified. The problem is that once you are sucked into such a game, it always seems to pay to spend a little more. This is often true in races for patents and innovations. Silicon Valley is full of exponents of chicken, and its investors are playing the same game.

Perhaps we should refuse to play chicken. Yet if you stay out of these games, you pass winning opportunities by. You can develop a strong position if you can make an irrevocable commitment. If you could tear off the steering wheel and throw it out the window, you would be a certain winner in *Rebel Without a Cause* or *Stand by Me*.

This is the paradox of Alexander the Great burning his boats, or Grant's attack on Vicksburg during the American Civil War. You can do better by restricting your options. If you can't quit, or risk losing a reputation as a stayer, you are a formidable opponent at chicken. That is how IBM won the standards battle in personal computers and why Rupert Murdoch has done so well in many of the markets he has entered.

But the greatest paradox of all is that it is often best to adopt random behaviour in chicken games. It is possible to write down the mathematics of the problem faced by the two groups of boys in *Stand by Me*, and to show that in general a good solution for each is to swerve sometimes and to stick sometimes. You can even calculate how often you should swerve and how often you should stick.

But how to decide which option to adopt? It's a mistake to rely on any objective criteria. If you did, then your opponent might guess how you made your decision, and act accordingly. I couldn't find a movie with the child's game of stone, scissors, paper, but it illustrates the point. Stone blunts scissors, but is wrapped by paper, while scissors cut paper. Any predictable behaviour loses this game, and randomness wins half the time against another random player. The only way to keep your strategy secret from others is not to know what it is yourself.

Now this is not a recommendation that business strategies should be based on the toss of a coin, although that might be safer than following the recommendations of many consultants. Not knowing may be better than knowing: random behaviour more profitable than rational analysis. Limiting your flexibility may yield higher payoffs, and you can lose far more from chicken games than you could ever hope to win. Learn to play chicken in business when you must, but learn from the adolescent rites of passage in *Rebel Without a Cause* and *Stand by Me* that it is usually better not to be playing these games at all.

# DIY economics

22 OCTOBER 2003

## PART I

Samuel Brittan calls it businessmen's economics. David Henderson, long an international civil servant, prefers DIY economics. Both refer to propositions which people who have practical knowledge but no qualifications in economics hold to be self-evident, but which are false. Countries would do better to export more and import less. New technology destroys jobs, and public spending on my projects not only helps me but creates jobs. Manufacturing is more important than other forms of economic activity. Business would benefit from lower interest rates. People who would pause before expressing opinions in quantum mechanics or undertaking brain surgery have no hesitation in pronouncing on the economic consequences of the euro.

DIY is not confined to economics, or carpentry. There is DIY medicine, and even DIY physics. Common sense tells us that heavier objects fall faster, the sun revolves round the earth, and the kitchen will be cooler if you leave the refrigerator door open. But experience is often misleading if we are not trained to interpret it. It is true that feathers and other light objects fall to the ground slowly, but we mistakenly infer a general rule. And we see the sun rise in the east and set in the west every day. It is so obvious that the sun circles the earth that people who denied it used to be burnt at the stake.

But we only observe part of the solar system, not the whole. When you study the interactions of moving planets you realise that orbits around the sun are a much more compelling way of understanding the universe. And when you open the fridge door,

A fundamental principle of economics is to follow your comparative advantage

you can feel the cold air. What you do not see is the chain of consequences. The compressor works continuously in an attempt to maintain the inside temperature, and the heat it ejects from the back of the fridge more than offsets the cold encountered at the front.

Scientific research and formal education are needed to understand complex systems. We learn very little about the economy by being consumers and producers, just as we do not become expert in aerodynamics as passengers in a plane. The fallacies of DIY economics are mostly the result of generalisation in which we mistakenly infer the properties of the whole from our limited experience of a smaller part.

Because every currency purchase must be matched by a sale, reducing imports has effects on exchange rates and on the output of other producers, just as opening the fridge door alerts the thermostat and triggers the compressor. New technology may displace labour from individual jobs, but enhances prices and profits and so increases demand for both the products of new technology and for unrelated goods. Interest rate cuts would be good for business if their only effect were to reduce borrowing costs. But there are many more extensive consequences of interest rate changes, and it is precisely because there are more extensive consequences that setting monetary policy is a challenging task. The complex range of goods and services we need is the product of our interdependent economy. Are the brakes of a car more important than the engine? To ask the question is to display profound ignorance of the automobile as complex system.

Airline passengers can usefully comment on the comfort or discomfort they experience, but do well to leave the design of the plane to aeronautical engineers. Businessmen can helpfully describe the effects of interest or exchange rates on their own business, but that defines the limit of what they can knowledgeably say.

Galileo climbed the leaning tower, not because he needed to check how quickly a lead weight would fall, but because it was the only way to convince the sceptical merchants of Pisa that gravity was not a purely theoretical construct. DIY economics persists, like DIY medicine, because there are rarely definite connections between causes and effects. If you get better after taking the snake oil, no one can tell whether it was the snake oil, or whether you would have got better anyway. Physicists are fortunate to have opportunities for decisive experiments: doctors and economists rarely have the chance. But even Galileo could not persuade the Inquisitors to look through his telescope, because ideology told them that what he claimed to see could not be there. It is a familiar experience in economic matters.

## PART 2

Since I warned against DIY economics – the false propositions that people who know little about economics think are true – my electronic mailbox has been filled by people who say they are sticking to DIY because they have been let down by cowboy tradesmen. Not dodgy decorators or crooked carpenters, but economic forecasters.

Most economists don't do forecasting, and like honest craftsmen they resent those who earn more money for shoddier work. Several decades ago, in the first flush of naive enthusiasm for the potential of computers, many people believed that large models would describe the evolution of the economy ever more perfectly. But these hopes were unfounded. It is not simply that economists are not sufficiently clever, or their tools not sufficiently powerful. Predicting whether the dollar will rise or fall in the second quarter of next year, or the level of the Standard & Poor's index at the end of 2004, is in principle impossible.

The reasons fall into two main groups. Many of the processes we find in commercial and economic life are dynamic and non linear. One implication for everyday life is that small differences in where you start can make a large difference to where you finish – the path dependency illustrated by the rule of the road (p 58). If small events can have large effects on complex systems, then even knowing 99% of what you need to know leaves you vulnerable to large errors. And 100% knowledge is impossible.

That is why we can never aspire to accurate forecasting of economic events, just as we can never know whether it will rain on June 4 next year or the date of the next Tokyo earthquake. But economics is even harder than meteorology or seismology. Most economic systems are reflexive – what happens is influenced by how we perceive what will happen. Good mechanisms for

ALL I'LL SAY IS, MAKE SURE YOU'RE INSURED AGAINST RANDOM AND TOTALLY UNPREDICTABLE EVENTS

forecasting stock prices will not be found because their very discovery would affect stock prices. If there had been reliable predictions that the value of the euro would move from $1.17 to 81c and back again, these movements would not have occurred.

But we can identify earthquake zones even if we cannot anticipate earthquakes: we can look forward to summer even if we cannot forecast the weather on 4 June next. Seismologists can tell us where not to build our houses, and meteorologists can help us know where to sell sun cream and when to take an umbrella. Useful economic knowledge is of a similar kind.

When the value of the euro fell below a dollar, it was virtually certain to appreciate, because it is rare for the currencies of rich countries to deviate so far from purchasing power parity (see p 37) for long. But no one could have successfully predicted just when the euro would appreciate, or that it would first fall to almost 80c: although the pattern of momentum in the short run and mean reversion in the long run is a common feature of speculative markets. And, in answer to the questions some readers may be asking: you need to take an economics course to learn about purchasing power parity and mean reversion, a physics course to learn about momentum, and yes, I did fill my boots with euros at an average price of 87c.

But, despite the inevitable failures of economic forecasting, people continue to want the knowledge it would provide. As even DIY economics will tell you, where there is demand there will be supply. Cowboy tradesmen remain in business because there are always gullible customers, and the same is true of economic forecasters.

But when someone tells you that the dollar will appreciate in the second quarter of next year, or what the level of S & P will be at the end of 2004, the only useful information they convey is that they don't know what they are talking about. If they did, they wouldn't be making these predictions. But if you stop asking economists to forecast the future, there are other interesting things they can tell you. I predict this column will appear again next week, and hope you will find something in it to enjoy.

---

In Britain, the term DIY is used for home improvements and hardware businesses are known as DIY stores: the acronym comes from a BBC television series with the title *Do It Yourself*.

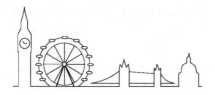

*Dear Sarah,*
*It was kind of you to write to say how much you enjoyed* The Truth about Markets, *and to ask whether you should contemplate a career as an economist.*

*Back in the 1960s, when I decided to take up the subject, economists were living in a golden age. The world economy had experienced two decades of unprecedented growth and stability. It seemed that Keynesian policies could cure unemployment and control the business cycle. Economics had become rigorous, mathematical, professional. Econometric models made it possible not just to forecast the future of economies and industries but to change these futures. Strategic planning was in vogue in government and business. Newly independent countries needed assistance to plan the development of their economies. There were jobs for economists everywhere.*

*When I was at school, economics was not an option that was offered. But soon bright young economics graduates entered teaching, and attracted good students. Economics quickly became one of the most popular school subjects, and university applications grew rapidly.*

*When I began teaching at Oxford, the most popular option was euphemistically described as the economics of developing countries: idealistic students hoped to learn how to end world poverty. But through the 1970s industrial organisation became their top choice. As jobs became harder to find, students wanted material that would help them in business.*

*But the stuff we taught in the developing countries option didn't do the countries it was supposed to help much good, and graduates* discovered that business wasn't interested in the industrial economics they had learned at university. Economics failed to match the public expectations it had created. Its prestige declined. Euphoria about government economic management evaporated with the oil shock and rising inflation and unemployment. The vogue for planning came to an end as management by numbers failed in business, in national economies, and on the battlefields of Vietnam.

The popularity of economics as a school and university subject peaked in the 1980s. Since then, the number of British students taking A level economics has fallen by almost half. The situation in universities is not so bad, partly because the big increase in number of students overall has kept numbers up, but the share of economics in the total has fallen rapidly. You will find it easier to get a place now than a few years ago.

When I graduated, there were opportunities for economists in universities, government and business, and most students ranked them in that order. The job market you will face will be very different. The traditional business economist has virtually disappeared. Once, most large companies had a chief economist with a staff, but almost none do today. Forecasts are not valued, and business economics is done, badly, by strategy people.

Almost the only firms which today employ economists are banks and securities houses. These people are not really wanted for their advice: they are entertainers who perform before clients and advertise their employers' services on breakfast television. Competition policy and privatisation created a new demand for economic expertise, to help companies deal with regulatory agencies. As you know, I spent several years building a consulting business specialising in these areas, and this and other firms still offer some interesting career opportunities.

Fewer good economists are attracted to government: the more ideological environment of the modern civil service marginalizes technical skills. Positions within the World Bank and International Monetary Fund, once highly prized, have become less attractive as these agencies have come under attack. It is not likely that you or

*anyone else in your class will be interested in an academic career. A
combination of low salaries and poor morale mean that for years now
almost no British students have taken PhDs at British universities.
The situation is not as bad in other countries, although it is still fairly
dire. You should expect that most junior lecturers in economics at a
British university will be from abroad, mainly Southern Europe.*

*If you go ahead with economics, your class will consist mainly of
boys. At every level, economics is one of the most male dominated
of academic subjects. I have to go and sign some more books now,
but I will write to you soon and try to explain why.*

*With love,*
*Uncle John*

12 June 2003                                              *Menton*

*Dear Sarah,*

*If you do go ahead and study economics, you will certainly meet
boys: two out of three A-level economics students are male. This is one
of the highest ratios of any subject. This gender bias goes right through
the profession. Most people studying economics at university are men.
Not one woman has yet received the Nobel Prize for economics. Some
people think that Joan Robinson, a Marxist and disciple of Keynes,
should have been a recipient. But she is probably the only woman
even to have been in contention. And perhaps the best known female
economist today is Deirdre McCloskey, a colourful figure who
pronounces on the rhetoric of economics, but who is still better known
to many from her earlier career as Donald McCloskey, economic
historian.*

*It is hard to argue that the economics profession discriminates
against women when male domination begins with the choices people
make at school. The causes seem more likely to lie in the nature of the
subject itself. When you start economics, you will be quickly*

introduced to rational economic man. It is always rational economic man, not rational economic woman, even in the most politically correct of classrooms. Rational economic man — self-absorbed, calculating, maximising — is recognisably a male stereotype.

Many students are repelled by the caricature of human behaviour that is rational economic man. And women more so than men. Your teachers insist that there is no difference between the nature of male and female intelligence, but most people know this is not true, and there is increasing scientific support for their beliefs. You should read Simon Baron-Cohen's new book The Essential Difference: his bold thesis is that the female brain is predominantly hard-wired for empathy, the male brain predominantly hard-wired for understanding and building systems.

If that argument is correct, it becomes easier to understand why more female students than male are drawn towards the social sciences: but, among those who are so attracted, women tend to do sociology and psychology and men economics. It takes a peculiar kind of personality to be interested in human behaviour, but have that interest satisfied by mathematical modelling. And that peculiar personality is more often found among men than women. The gender bias in economics should be set against the opposite bias in psychology.

So your classes will be full of men. Whether they are the men you would want to meet, I am less certain: experiments have found that students of economics conform much more closely to the behaviour of rational economic man than students of other subjects. Some economists have offered evolutionary explanations of why it makes sense to use this creature as the centrepiece of these models — they claim that rational economic man predominates because he would triumph in the survival of the fittest. You will have your own chance to participate in natural selection but rational economic man does not recognise affection, and I suspect he is not much fun to live with. One of the more apt jokes about economists is that an economist is someone who knows sixty-nine ways of making love, but no women.

Some argue that we need feminist economics. At first sight, this sounds as silly as the idea that we need feminist physics, but it is not quite as silly. The speed of light ought to be more or less the same whether it is measured by a man or a woman. Many economists imagine that they are searching for fundamental empirical truths about the world, like physicists measuring the speed of light. But more thoughtful economists realise that economic understanding is only one means of interpreting social phenomena. There can be no single explanation of how events like the recent stock market bubble came into being: any satisfactory account will want to draw not only on a variety of economic models but on insights from psychology – and even literature and epidemiology.

I suspect that economics will be more eclectic in the next fifty years than the last: the fixation of the profession with rational economic man will decline. Women should therefore be able to make a larger contribution in future than they have been allowed to make in the past and the subject will be richer for it. Perhaps you can help provide more empathy and less system building.

*Best wishes,*
*Uncle John*

# The Truth about Markets

2003

In the 1980s America won the cold war. In 1989 the Berlin Wall fell. The decade that followed proved one of the most extraordinary periods in economic history. The American business model – the unrestrained pursuit of self interest, market fundamentalism, the minimal state and low taxation – offered its followers the same certainties that Marxism had given its own adherents for the previous century. There was a New Economy.

It was all to end in a frenzy of speculation, followed by recrimination and self-doubt. Corporations that had never earned a cent of profit, and never would, were sold to investors for billions of dollars. Corporate executives would fill their pockets and invent revenues and profits to support their accounts of their own genius. And every international economic meeting would be besieged by demonstrators.

This ambitious and wide-ranging book unravels the truth about markets. Market economies function because they are embedded in a social, political and cultural context, and cannot work otherwise. These links explain why market economies outperformed socialist or centrally directed ones, but also why the imposition of market institutions often fails. Illustrated with examples from the shores of Lake Zürich to the streets of Mumbai, through evolutionary psychology and moral philosophy, to the flower market at San Remo and Christies' saleroom in New York. *The Truth about Markets* examines the big questions of economics – why some countries and people are rich, and others poor, why businesses succeed and fail, the scope of markets, and their limits.

# REVIEWS

'An ambitious and brilliantly executed book.' Richard Lambert, *The Times*

'John Kay's book explains some of the major economic topics of our time – indeed of all time.' Joseph Stiglitz, Nobel Prize Laureate in Economics, 2001

'A landmark work.' Will Hutton, *Management Today*

'This is quite possibly the only book on economics you will ever need to read.' Stefan Stern, *Accounting and Business*

'It offers one of the most truthful and fruitful ways in years of looking at the relationship between modern government and the modern economy.' Martin Kettle, *The Guardian*

'Written with wit and subtlety.' Martin Van der Weyer, *The Daily Telegraph*

'A comprehensive, well-structured and highly readable exploration of markets and how they work.' *The Scotsman*

'A welcome antidote to the one-dimensional, reductionist accounts of the business world.' Simon Caulkin, *The Observer*

'John Kay provides a remarkable explanation of difficult ideas in simple and clear language – everything you wanted to know about economics but were afraid to ask.' Mervyn King, Governor of the Bank of England.

A revised version was published in the United States in 2004 under the title *Culture and Prosperity*.

# Foundations of Corporate Success

1993

This book addresses the most fundamental of business issues – what makes a successful company? How did BMW recover from the edge of bankruptcy to become one of Europe's strongest companies? What lies behind the continuing success of companies like Sainsbury's, Marks and Spencer, and Reuters? Why did Saatchi and Saatchi's global strategy bring the company to its knees?

Drawing on his own business experience and on concepts in economics, legal theory, and sociology, John Kay argues that the answer lies in the distinctive capabilities of the organisation.

Hailed by critics when first published in 1993, this was the only business book by a British author chosen by the *Financial Times* in its Books of the Year List.

## REVIEWS

'one of the most important "strategic thinking" books in years...' *The Director*

'A fresh and insightful approach, blending theory and case studies, to the links between corporate culture, strategy and success.' Sir Geoffrey Owen, former editor of the *Financial Times*

'A major *tour de force* that should be read with diligence and inwardly digested...' *Economic Affairs*

'For a long time, I and other colleagues have looked for a book on business strategy which we could recommend unreservedly to MBA and final year undergraduate students. In Kay's book we have found one.' *Books for MBAs*

'... well on the way to becoming a European Michael Porter.' *The Economist*

# The Business of Economics

1996

Essays by John Kay on economics and business, 1990-96

Introduction

# www.johnkay.com

This website is a comprehensive guide to John Kay's activities and writing. On it you can:

- read and download a wide range of John Kay's articles

- search for materials on selected subjects

- receive advance notice of new publications

- order existing publications

- learn about current and coming events involving the author

- discover what is currently on John Kay's bookshelves

- obtain biographical and career details

# Beyond the bean and the cod

NOVEMBER 2005

*So this is good old Boston*
*The home of the bean and the cod*
*Where the Lowells talk only to Cabots*
*And the Cabots talk only to God*

In 1811 Francis Cabot Lowell, son of Susan Cabot and Judge John
Lowell, visited Europe. The wars which had engaged Europe since
the French revolution were approaching their climax in
Napoleon's disastrous invasion of Russia, and would soon ignite
conflict between Britain and the United States. Lowell's hosts
suspected he was a spy, restricted his movements and searched his
belongings.

Their suspicions were well founded. Lowell was indeed a spy
but he was engaged in industrial rather than military espionage.
His purpose was to apply in Massachusetts the technology and
principles of business organisation he had observed in Europe.
The Boston Company, established in 1813, implemented new
technology, raised capital, constructed an integrated production
system, managed relations with customers and suppliers, and
recruited a disciplined labour force. The Boston Company was
America's first modern business enterprise, and Lowell was the
first of America's great industrialists.

But Lowell and his associates feared that the urban squalor,
immorality and conflict he had observed in Europe would
undermine America's fledgling democracy and the Puritan virtues
which underpinned the society they led. At Waltham the Boston
Company built not just a mill, but a company town. It regulated

not only the working conditions of its employees but almost every aspect of their lives. The Waltham system was most extensively developed at Lowell, the town named for Francis after his death. When Charles Dickens, relentlessly hostile to the consequences of England's industrial revolution, visited Lowell, he was effusive in his praise.

Lowell had instinctively appreciated that the modern business enterprise would change the nature of the society in which it operated, and that the nature of the society in which it operated would determine the performance of the enterprise. What obligations went with the considerable powers of modern managers – and what were the proper limits of these powers? Most fundamentally, what was the nature and basis of management authority in a democracy where the exercise of power is ultimately subject to a process of election?

These issues would recur in many different contexts in the two centuries that followed. Marx asserted that the question 'what makes management power legitimate?' had no persuasive answer, and that resistance to that power would ultimately destroy the capitalist system itself. Almost a century later, in 1946, Peter Drucker would write the first business book, *The Concept of the Corporation*. Drucker's subject was the nature of the professionally managed business and its relationship to its political and cultural context.

Drucker's case study was the archetype of modern business organisation – General Motors. Half a century later, the Detroit automobile manufacturer is neither particularly successful nor typical of the modern business enterprise. There have been many changes to the environment within which companies operate, the product of globalisation and new technology, the issue of the scope and nature of the corporation remains a live issue as the political and business context in which it is conducted changes. Conflicting claims are made of the need for corporate social responsibility and the primacy of shareholder value, and there are simultaneous demands for tighter regulation of business activity and the introduction of private sector efficiencies into the public sector.

The business of business is business. It is not narrower than this. Business organisations are not purely instrumental, their business objectives ancillary to an underlying financial purpose. And to treat them as such not only undermines the legitimacy of capitalism as a system but reduces the effectiveness of the corporations themselves. But business organisations do not have a wider role: they have neither an obligation to promote social welfare, nor a right to pursue any particular conception of what social welfare might be. Successful corporations have identities, even personalities of their own. Reductionist views, which look through corporations and see only contracts between individuals, omit the fundamental reasons why such business organisations exist.

These propositions may seem obvious. But they are radically at variance with much current thinking. And they have extensive implications, both for public policy towards business and for the management of corporations themselves....

---

This is edited from the introduction to John Kay's next book which draws on and extends the ideas in *Foundations of Corporate Success (Why Firms Succeed)* and *The Truth about Markets (Culture and Prosperity)*. The book is currently scheduled for publication in late 2005. For information on progress and for up-to-date information on publication date, pricing and availability, go to www.johnkay.com